COUNTRY HOUSE
GARDEN

COUNTRY HOUSE GARDEN

DAVID HATCHETT

35 line illustrations by Rosemary Wise
60 black and white photographs

DAVID & CHARLES
Newton Abbot   London   North Pomfret (Vt)

British Library Cataloguing in Publication Data

Hatchett, David
   Country house garden
   1. Gardening – England – Cornwell (Oxfordshire)
   I. Title
   635'.09425'71   SB98

   ISBN 0-7153-8250-0

Typeset by Typesetters (Birmingham) Ltd, Smethwick
and printed in Great Britain
by Butler & Tanner Ltd, London and Frome
for David & Charles (Publishers) Limited
Brunel House   Newton Abbot   Devon

Published in the United States of America
by David & Charles Inc
North Pomfret   Vermont 05053   USA

CONTENTS

INTRODUCTION

The village of Cornwell lies in the centre of a triangle of three North Cotswold market towns. Standing nearly 150m (500ft) high, surrounded on three sides by rolling hills of up to 250m (800ft), it is open only to the south-west, where runs the Evenlode Valley. The village itself nestles on the side of a deeply cut chine, through which flows a tributary brook of the Evenlode, its source a mere 100 metres from the stone cottages. Just how long this spring has been here is very difficult to say, but as Cornwell was mentioned in the Domesday Book and more than likely derives its name from Corne-well, one must presume it was there in those days and probably many years before that.

We know for certain that the village has been sited in at least two different areas within an 800 metre (half mile) square, and proof of this can be readily seen. Today's village consists of eleven cottages, of which four, including mine, are Jacobean and built of Taynton stone. The other seven were added at a later date, as were the schoolhouse and shop which we know to be Victorian. The shop has been closed some years, and the schoolhouse is now the estate office.

A little further east stands Cornwell Manor, commanding a fine view of the valley, and 400 metres beyond lies the Norman church of St Peter. The manor house has been dated to around 1640, but a study of the cellars and a turret has led to the opinion that some parts could be two hundred years earlier.

In 1937, Mrs Anthony Gillson, a wealthy American lady, bought the estate consisting of village, manor house, farms and surrounding lands. At that time many of the cottages were in a poor state of repair, and the garden as we know it today did not exist. Through her generosity and concern Cornwell, to quote from an article written in 1939, was rescued from becoming a 'derelict hamlet'. She engaged the services of a famous architect, the late Clough Williams-Ellis of Portmeirion fame, whose first task was to rebuild where necessary and modernise the existing cottages.

The south wall of the manor house. Conifers and young spring foliage of willow and acer are reflected in the central reservation of the canal

The old village school, now the estate office

It was also at this time that thoughts were turned to the garden, and one of the country's leading landscape contractors, Wm Wood & Son of Taplow, was brought in to design and construct the major features to be seen to this day. The contractors' skilful use of existing water that ran through the garden, the building of the rock and bog garden, and the planting of trees, shrubs and hedging is a constant reminder of their craft.

Like many other big houses during the war, Cornwell Manor was used as a convalescent home, in this case for the Women's Forces. After the war the estate was sold, and for the next twelve years Lord and Lady Crighton-Stewart resided at the Manor. In 1959 the estate was acquired by the present owner, the Hon Peter Ward, and in the following years a considerable amount of formal terracing was added to the sloping lawns and many ornamental trees and bulbs were planted.

THE VEGETABLE GARDEN

The ½ hectare (1¼ acre) garden is bordered on three sides by a stone wall 3m (10ft) high, and on the fourth side by a thick yew hedge. As well as offering some protection from the cold wind, the walls provide an ideal setting for trained fruit trees. At the same time, a walled garden such as this can act as a frost pocket, and on numerous occasions I have seen early morning frosts literally rolling over these walls; but to compensate, it can be a sun trap in the summer.

The vegetable garden is labour intensive, but full of character, and we try to keep it as an integral part of the gardens and not a 'plot of ground behind a wall for growing vegetables'. Photographs of it in 1938 show topiary yew hedges bordering the growing areas, lavish flower beds and even a pool and fountain, but in those days there were twelve gardeners. These features have long since gone, but there still remains an air of the old-fashioned garden.

From a wrought iron gate in the lower wall the garden is divided by a stone path with grass borders, which leads to a small stone building that was once an apple store. Two lateral paths run across, dividing the whole garden into approximately six equal areas. One of these is grassed down and planted with young apple trees on dwarf stock. A further sixth is a fruit cage, which was in an appalling mess when I first came to Cornwell. Weeds of every description had completely taken over, but now I am thankful to say this area is again productive. This leaves me with just over 3,000 sq m (¾ acre) on which to grow fresh vegetables all year for twelve people.

Along the south-facing wall there are sixteen fan-trained plums, mainly Victoria, plus an old fig tree which although not very productive, I have not the heart to remove. Across the top wall we have nearly seventy cordon pears and one very old espalier pear, Pitmaston Duchess, tucked into the corner by the tool shed. The bottom wall is home for a further ten espalier pears on one side of the path and blackcurrants on the other side.

Standard apple trees are grown on both sides of the central path at the top and bottom, and midway is an avenue of espalier pears. Doors in the long wall lead out to an old orchard and the tennis court, whilst two wrought iron gates in the bottom wall take us through to the pavilion and the swimming pool. Grass paths border the trained fruit and the central path – a lot of work indeed to keep cut and tidy, before one's thoughts can turn to the actual growing of vegetables. As for the future – who knows? But I hope that we shall always be able to maintain this part of the garden to a high standard.

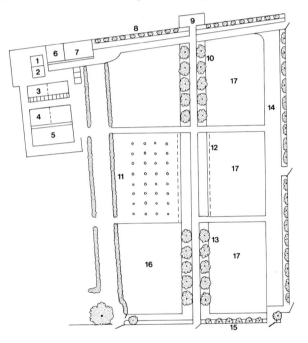

The vegetable garden and greenhouses: **1** Boiler-house; **2** Office; **3** Propagating house and frames; **4** Plant house; **5** Tomato house; **6** Pot store; **7** Tool shed; **8** Cordon-trained pears; **9** Cloche and sundries store; **10** Apple – Cox's Orange Pippin; **11** Bush apples on dwarf stock; **12** Espalier-trained pears; **13** Apple – Bramley Seedling; **14** Fan-trained plums and gages; **15** Trained pears; **16** Soft fruit cage; **17** Growing areas

Looking across the young orchard to the greenhouses, with gardeners' and gamekeeper's cottages in the background

THE GREENHOUSES

The greenhouse, above all, must give the professional gardener immense interest and satisfaction. It is a necessity in a large garden, providing the medium for raising and propagating plants of all kinds, yet an expensive one with the high cost of maintenance and even higher cost of fuel oil.

The site where the greenhouses now stand was once an old nut orchard that sloped away to the cottages. The area has been made up and retained by stone walls, keeping it at the same height as the vegetable garden, and is protected by yew hedging.

The original two greenhouses were designed and built by Wm Wood & Son in 1938. The firm's name is cast into the metal eave and ridge supports, a constant reminder of their craftsmanship. The smaller house is 12m (40ft) in length and 3.5m (12ft) wide, 1.5m (5ft) to the eaves, and built on a 75cm (2ft 6in) brick base. As well as having doors at both ends, it is centrally divided by a glass partition and door, making it two greenhouses in one as it were. I think the divider is essential, making the control of temperature and humidity a separate task for each half, as well as providing ease of fumigation. Roof and side ventilators are operated from a worm drive at each end, and benching 75cm (2½ft) high by 105cm (3½ft) wide runs the full length each side. Benching is covered with pea gravel as is the floor space beneath, and a concrete path from door to door gives a clean and manageable finish. Ample guttering takes rainwater to two tanks built into the sides at ground level.

The addition of a soil warming bench, heating some 3.7sq m (40sq ft) has made us less reliant on normal pipe heat, and is in fact an essential item for seed raising and propagation. The cable lies in clean grit sand which is covered with fine polythene, minimising heat loss, but it is of utmost importance that the sand is kept uniformly moist to run the unit economically.

Outside, a row of frames has been built on to the east-facing wall of the house, and these are used mainly for hardening off bedding subjects as well as protecting young or tender plants during the winter, the cooler, airy conditions being much to the liking of many plants. The ventilation is controlled by a metal bar fixed to each frame and slotted into any one of ten teeth on the light, giving a firm hold on openings from 10cm (4in) to maximum. It is the first time that I have encountered this method, and I wonder why it is not used more nowadays, as it affords a practical and easy way of frame management.

The second greenhouse is what I call a 'gentleman's' house, purpose built for the growing of a very wide range of plants. Again built on a 75cm (2ft 6in) brick base, it is 12m (40ft) long and 6m (20ft) wide, necessitating a ridge height of 3.3m (11ft). As in the smaller greenhouse there are doors at each end and a glass divider. As well as benching 75cm (2ft 6in) wide at the side and ends, there are additional table benches 4.5m (15ft) by 1.8m (6ft) either side of the partition. In a house of this size, it is very easy to rearrange benching to individual requirements, and in most cases fixtures and roof brackets were built into the original structure. Side and roof ventilators run the full length of the house, and adequate rainwater storage is built in under the central staging. What a pleasure it is to work in a greenhouse such as this, with plenty of height above one's head, roomy, easy to manage and with a growing atmosphere.

The third house was added in 1966 and is a further span of similar dimensions built on to the second house. Primarily for tomatoes, it is simply constructed without frills, strong and sensibly ventilated. The floor area is concrete except for a soil border 1.2m (4ft) wide on the east side, not the best conditions one would think, for the production of tomatoes, but as this area is all made up with hardcore and subsoil, we have to grow the crop in large pots.

All three structures are timber built, and although they require considerably more maintenance than modern aluminium ones, I think they are less prone to sudden temperature changes and retain a little more warmth on winter days. They are heated by 10cm (4in)

Cream teas served on the terrace at the church fête

hot water pipes, fed by an oil fired boiler at the rear of the potting shed. The system is a luxurious one, designed in the days when any fuel was a cheap commodity, but with rise in prices over the last three years, it is now very debatable whether oil or solid fuel is cheaper. With the added labour costs that solid fuel entails, I think oil must still have the edge. Apart from setting thermostats to the required temperature, everything is automatic, clean and efficient.

We heat our houses from late October until early May, but with the present high costs we have reduced the minimum temperature from 13°C (55°F) to 4.5°C (40°F), and what were 'warm' houses in winter have now become 'cool' houses. Nevertheless, the range of plants we grow is still wide, though flowering times are later, and the change in environment presents a constant challenge to even the most experienced of plantsmen.

THE GARDEN

Of the 2 hectares (5 acres) of ornamental garden that I and my staff look after, a fairly big proportion lies as an L-shaped block on the south- and east-facing sides of the manor house. Perhaps some of this area cannot really be classed as ornamental, being semi-woodland, yet in its own way it is one of the most charming parts of

13

the garden. At this stage I wish only to create a picture in the reader's eye of the main features and layout. The entrance to Cornwell Manor faces south, and opens on to a terrace that runs the full length of the house and extends nearly twenty metres into the garden. The terrace is contained on three sides by stone balustrading 60cm (2ft) high, opening to wide steps that lead down to the main lawn. The lawn slopes gently away to a grass bank and the croquet lawn, on the far side of which runs the spring water from the top of the village. After running through the gardens of the lower cottages and fording its way across our access road, the stream continues into an old orchard, and from here on we can see how Clough Williams-Ellis used it to create the garden's main feature. He cleverly canalised it all the way to the head of the rock garden before allowing the water to run through in informal surroundings.

Passing under the main drive, it emerges through a stone tunnel to drop 1m (3ft) before continuing along the narrow canal, the only diversion from the straight being a circular opening forming part of the view from the terrace. The eye is held as it passes across the water and up a series of stone terraced steps and grass terraces to a fine wrought iron gate.

At the lower end of the canal the lawn drops steeply away into the valley, and it is on this slope that the rock garden was constructed. It consists of numerous outcrops of Westmorland stone, connected by a series of three small pools through which runs the water of the canal. Small waterfalls divert the flow from outcrop to pool, but as at certain times of the year there is more water than they can comfortably handle, the surplus is diverted under ground to emerge through a stone-sided gulley and over a number of steps before joining the flow from the rock garden.

Running now for a further hundred metres over a stony bed to form the bog garden, the stream passes under a stone bridge and is met by other outlets of spring water before tumbling into the first of three lakes and eventually finding its way to the Evenlode.

We have done considerable work on the rock and water garden during the last three years, bringing it into closer harmony with the surroundings, and providing great interest as well as a diversity of plant and animal life.

'The Fiddler' stands against a background of weeping pears and steps up to the Spring garden

Rose beds and a newly planted shrub border run along the base of the terrace followed by twin herbaceous borders at the foot of a stone wall; steps up lead to the formal garden. It is only in the last twenty-five years that this feature has been added – stone retaining walls and steps leading to three terraces, charming in their own way and with a magnificent view across the valley.

Steps up, yet again, take us back to informality in the shape of the Spring garden, an area devoted to naturalised bulbs and dominated by a huge beech, its overhang of branches providing dappled shade to the delight of all the plants that grow beneath.

There are no boundary fences on this east side, no feeling of containment as the garden merges gently into surrounding farmland with only a ha-ha to keep the sheep at bay.

The remainder of the garden is as different again for, with the building of many metres of stone walling and the planting of a similar length of yew hedges, numerous small gardens have been formed, secluded corners, sheltered walls both sunny and shaded, providing us with a choice and the means to grow a wide selection of lime-tolerant plants.

THE SOIL

It is not the easiest of tasks to describe the land in general of the North Cotswolds. In this garden alone we have depths of soil varying from 7.5cm (3in) to little more than 30cm (1ft), and within a distance of 30 metres the texture can change dramatically. Perhaps not, one would think, the best medium for growing vegetables, flowers, trees and shrubs. Yet with an understanding of the land plus – the most important point of all – the addition of organic material and a little help from nature, it is possible to achieve very satisfactory results. We are of course in limestone country, where the soil lies over varying depths of oolite, or brash as we prefer to call it, and in many cases a solid rock bed. Indeed, we are fortunate that the list of lime-loving plants is almost endless, and the sight of them revelling in what seems a stony dustiness must warm the heart of any plantsman. Soil tests that I have taken during the last year have resulted in pH readings of 6.7 to 7.3, not as high in some cases as

Clipped yews, alstroemerias and lavenders on the lower terrace, with small standard trees of *Prunus lusitanica*

one would expect, in fact, approaching neutral in some areas.

This widens even further the range of plants that can be grown successfully, a challenge to the ambitious gardener. In summer the land can be warm, with large stones working their way to the surface and the texture apparently dry. In winter it is often cold, a wet unmanageable sticky mess. Gardening is all about observation, when and where to plant, and in the following chapters I hope to pass on helpful information that I have gained from experience.

THE GARDEN STAFF

Stuart is a dedicated horticulturist, knowledgeable in all aspects and possessing an eye for detail so essential in private gardening.

John, who recently joined us, has a degree in economics and has abandoned city life for a career in gardening.

Norman is semi-retired, a countryman with a lifetime of farming experience, pursuing his great interest, vegetables.

The canal tunnel

JANUARY

Here in the Cotswolds this is perhaps not the coldest month of the year, but it is certainly the most unpredictable. Depending on the direction of the wind we can expect gales and prolonged rain from the west, snow showers from the north and severe cold weather from the east. Seldom are two days the same, making the allocation of work around the garden a day-to-day task, and only by accepting and working with the weather can we hope to use the winter days to our best advantage. It is the month for cold fingertips in the grey early morning, for piling on warm clothing and for the almost continuous use of rubber boots. The shortest day has passed and we look forward to the lengthening evenings.

Against an evening sky the outline and shape of the trees, both in the garden and surrounding parkland, are never more clearly defined than they are this month, and only two years after their disappearance I find it almost impossible to remember where the elms once stood. The lawns and grass fields have mellowed in colour and all around us there seems no urgency to grow and survive.

The vegetable garden as always continues to provide us with an enormous amount of work, but thankfully, due to a kind autumn, all the winter digging possible has been completed. This area amounting to about 2000sq m (½ acre) is given heavy dressings of compost and well rotted farmyard manure before being hand dug by Norman. He has a steady rhythmic action, like a well oiled machine, pausing only to clean off the spade at the end of a row.

I have always firmly believed that the addition of organic material to the soil is of utmost importance, and on this shallow Cotswold land it is an absolute necessity. Whilst we compost all organic waste from the garden, and it is a considerably large amount, the end product falls far short of our total requirements. We are fortunate indeed that during the winter months we have a continuous supply of strawy horse manure from nearby stables, and it is our first task every morning to collect and stack this valuable material. You may wonder just how and where large quantities of compost can be

A winter morning on the upper lake

produced, but in one of the outside orchards stand the base walls of an old greenhouse 18m (60ft) long by 6m (20ft) wide, which provides us with an excellent ready-made site. The horse manure is stacked separately, kept moist, and covered with black polythene sheeting, retaining the heat that is generated and also preventing winter rains washing away valuable minerals. It is not uncommon to see a fox resting on the top of this heap enjoying the warmth on a cold day.

The garden is still very productive, and we have a fine batch of leeks this season. Lifting begins in early December, the variety being Autumn Mammoth, and these take us through to February when Winter Reuzen is reaching its best. This is a first-class table leek, short and thick with large dark green leaves, of excellent flavour, and our bed of two hundred is soon depleted. The bulk of cabbage Christmas Drumhead has been cut and January King will fill the gap for a week or two. Celtic follows, an FI Hybrid of Scottish origin and hardy enough to stand the worst of weather. Its one fault is perhaps that I find it rather lacking in flavour, and I may try another variety next winter.

The last decade has seen great advances in the breeding of hybrid Brussels sprouts, and by trial and error I have found that Peer Gynt comes out top for quality and quantity on our particular land. For early work it is completely reliable, standing well and retaining firm buttons over a long season. To follow I grow a row each of Citadel and Ladora, both producing medium-sized dark green sprouts, with

Ladora maturing a little later to provide a succession.

I have given up storing carrots; a few weeks out of the ground renders them soft and tasteless—or perhaps my storing methods are at fault. For a late crop I sow Autumn King in July and August, and if the land is in good heart by October it is making quite heavy stump-ended carrots. These we lift through the winter, earthing up a little extra soil over the shoulders to protect them from sharp frosts. Losses are fairly high, both from heavy rain and slugs, but the survivors are sweet and well textured.

The same goes for beetroot, and a late sowing of Boltardy provides me with medium-sized roots until well past Christmas, but unfortunately this year the squirrels have taken a liking to them and I may have to protect them in future seasons. Spinach beet still pushes up a few succulent leaves after being cut down in October, and makes a welcome change from brassicas.

Hard as we may try, we just cannot grow table-quality celery in this garden. The wet texture of the soil overlying limestone is not conducive to the success of this crop, and without going to great lengths to remove the brash and import soil, we must be satisfied with second-class heads, most of which are destined for the soup pot. One root crop we do store is celeriac. The roots are lifted in late October and boxed in dry sand, providing us with an excellent ingredient for soup as well as being delicious cut thinly and fried.

The mild spell of weather in late autumn has encouraged the sprouting broccoli and spring heading cauliflowers to make soft growth, and I hope the sharp frosts will halt them in their tracks. Frost is vital to the winter-dug ground, for without it we have no means of producing a tilth in the early spring.

Aquadulce Claudia broad beans, sown in November, are sturdy and not too advanced; they must be the only variety that can truly stand winter conditions. Alas, I cannot say the same for the autumn-sown peas Feltham First; December rains have taken their toll and mice have feasted on the remainder. They are a gamble when all is said and done, a welcome bonus if they do survive. But having had only one successful crop in five years I think my future policy will be to sow in early March under cloches.

I like to complete the pruning of apples and pears by the end of the month, but with other work pressing I have yet to make a start and now it must be a priority. The seventy cordon and thirty espalier pears are the most important, but as they were summer pruned the previous August the task is considerably easier now. The summer pruning consisted of shortening the current season's growth to five leaves from the base, this controlling vigour, encouraging the formation of fruit buds and allowing the maximum amount of sunshine to reach the fruit. All that remains now is to cut back the laterals and thin out overcrowded spurs. On limestone canker is always prevalent, and the cutting out of diseased wood and painting over of cuts and wounds will help to minimise the disease. Cordons are kept down to 3m (10ft) in height; varieties include Doyenné du Comice, Durondeau, Beurré Hardy, Williams' Bon Chrétien and Joséphine de Malines. Espaliers are limited to four spans, trained on wires between oak posts, and are mainly Conference. Many of these trees are thirty or more years old and continue to produce good crops of fruit every year.

Apples we have an abundance of, the most recent planting consisting of forty bushes on dwarf stock, a mixture of dessert apples and cookers producing the quality fruit for table use and storage. Pruning is largely a matter of shape and size and I use the renewal system to keep a balance of shoot growth and fruit bud formation. Worcester Pearmain, Spartan, Winston and Golden Delicious are among the dessert varieties, while Golden Noble and the huge Howgate Wonder provide for the kitchen.

The standard trees at either end of the garden path are Cox's Orange Pippin and Bramley Seedling. We prune the Cox fairly hard every other year, but I find that to produce quality fruit a feeding programme is necessary as well as irrigation in a dry summer. On the other hand the Bramley, with its spreading branches, is a shade too vigorous for its position, and requires very hard pruning to keep it in hand. It is probably the most widely grown cooking apple of all, understandably so, as its heavy cropping and rich flavour plus excellent keeping qualities make it a natural choice – but it must be given space.

Soft fruit pruning is almost completed with the exception of gooseberries, which we leave until next month. Where possible I remove about one third of the blackcurrants' old fruiting wood to ground level, keeping the bush open and well furnished with young growth. We grow the early Boskoop Giant, Wellington XXX and Baldwin for mid-season picking, and Amos Black for a late crop. Red and white currants require rather different treatment: as most of the fruit is borne on short spurs on older wood the leading shoots need shortening by half and weaker growth cut back to three eyes. All currants respond to feeding, and a top dressing of farmyard manure in winter is very beneficial. Nitrogen deficiency is often the cause of poor quality fruit, and an application of a balanced fertiliser will usually correct this, and on no account should they go short of water in a dry season.

I like to check over the cane fruit now and make sure that all ties are secure before the snow arrives. Raspberries in particular are very prone to wind and snow damage, and it is essential that young canes are firmly tied.

Apart from the fruit trees in the kitchen garden we have three other orchards in varying parts of the garden. They consist mainly of old apple trees, many of which are past their prime, but one or two varieties such as Beauty of Bath, Ellison's Orange and Laxton's Superb bear reasonable fruit on the high branches. We have time only to remove diseased wood, and in the future I see the role of these trees as ornamental more than productive, playing host to the large drifts of daffodils planted beneath.

One of the more pleasant tasks for this month is the ordering of seeds and bulbs. I prefer to do this at home by the warmth of a fire with the numerous catalogues I receive laid out in front of me for comparison. Vegetable seeds are bought wholesale in bulk and consist of varieties that I know from experience will suit our land. As well as flower seeds to produce a year-round display in the greenhouse, I like to have a few packets of hardy and half-hardy annuals, both as gap-fillers in the borders and for filling numerous stone troughs and urns. For this I rely on old favourites such as godetia Sybil Sherwood, nigella Miss Jekyll, plus the two excellent lavateras of recent introduction, Silver Cup and Mont Blanc.

Most of the garden is permanently planted, and consequently we do very little bedding out, the exception being a circular bed in the swimming pool area.

The stocks of sundry items must also be checked – fertilisers, fumigants, insecticides, tying materials, tools – and ordered where necessary. Shears, grass-cutting machinery and mechanical implements must be sharpened and serviced, seed trays and plant pots washed clean. Cloche glass must be wiped over and replaced where broken, secateurs and knives and sickles honed, trailer wheels greased, potting soil mixed – and then some of my friends say, 'What on earth do you do in the winter?'

Under glass this is an important month, as rainy days will probably allow us some time to clean the greenhouses thoroughly. Roofing glass is wiped over with warm water to which soft soap and a dash of Jeyes Fluid has been added, and loose putty replaced. It is amazing just how much rubbish can accumulate both on the bench top and under the staging in the course of a year, and by running the pea gravel through a riddle we remove dead leaves and soil. Wooden staging is given a coat of preservative and the brick base walls are washed down with an algicide. To carry out all this work I empty the house of all plants, and ventilate it well before returning them.

The thermostat is set for a minimum night temperature of 4.5°C (40°F), excluding all frost and giving us a few extra degrees of growing atmosphere. When I first came to Cornwell we ran a minimum winter temperature of 13°C (55°F), allowing us to grow a very wide range of plants throughout the winter, including orchids. The high cost of heating oil has caused us to economise, the reduction in temperature forcing us to adapt and learn new methods of growing. With the bonus of occasional winter sunshine, day temperatures can soar to 13°C (55°F) or more, but I believe that careful ventilation to keep the temperature down to 10°C (50°F), reducing the fluctuation to a minimum, results in much healthier plants.

Of course, the keynote to success is watering; too little will severely check the plant, too much is a killer, and only by careful observation and knowledge of the species grown can the amount be correctly determined. The removal of dead leaves and the control of aphids is also all important, and if feeding is necessary it must be at half strength.

Many bulbs and corms such as achimenes, begonias, gloxinias and smithianthas are now completely dormant and should remain absolutely dry in their pots under the staging.

Although there is a general air of rest in the greenhouses this month, we are able to supply a good number of pot plants in flower to the manor house. Cinerarias are among the best I have ever grown, the cooler temperature being obviously to their liking. The strain is Hybrida Grandiflora with beautifully zoned flowers in a wide range of colours, individual blooms measuring up to 7.5cm (3in) across. Raised from seed last June and stood in an open shaded frame all summer, they are indispensable in the cool house from December onwards. Primulas are well represented by *malacoides, stellata, sinensis* and *kewensis* varieties. I can never understand why *P. kewensis* is not more widely grown, it is almost hardy and its fragrant buttercup-yellow flowers in whorls remain with us for many weeks. *P. malacoides* and *P. stellata* are showing their first flowers, but *P. obconica* and *P. sinensis* would be happier with a little more warmth, and we shall see how they fare.

We have a number of plants of *Azalea indica* which are at least fifteen years old, but gnarled and misshapen as they are, they continue to flower abundantly. Grown in large pots and re-potted annually after flowering, they disprove the fact that they need higher temperatures. Standing outside facing north during the summer and watered only with rainwater, they enjoy a buoyant atmosphere on their return under glass. Other plants in flower include the solanum Red Giant, its red berries just colouring up, *Browallia speciosa major* and the last of the *Exacum affine*.

My wren is back, visiting me in the propagating house, her presence given away only by the slight movement of a leaf. She stays until mid-February before leaving to nest in the yew hedge.

Complain as we do about rainfall, a high proportion of the lawns we see today are testimony to the suitability of our climate to grow grass. A well-kept lawn, regularly cut and with neat edges, will considerably enhance its surroundings, but let it once get out of hand and we see the character of the garden completely changed. In many instances the lawn extends right up to the house, and there is much to recommend this feature as long as planting is kept in close harmony.

I had made up my mind at Christmas that, time and weather permitting, we would endeavour to improve the condition of cylinder-mown lawns, and especially the croquet lawn. Moss has always been a problem here, as the lawn is partially shaded and lies close to water. However, I'm sure that the main cause is that there is a 10cm (4in) layer of topsoil over the brash, so that the lawn becomes quickly impoverished, and regular dressings of fertiliser are needed to keep the fine grasses growing strongly.

Preparatory work is all important and on these counts I may be old fashioned, but I still think that the use of the wire rake, besom and hollow-tined fork are superior to any machine. Of course, we all know that a dressing of moss-killer will do the job, but it does not remove the bed of dead grass formed after a season's mowing, nor does it allow air to get to the roots, and in many cases it is poisonous to bird life.

This is not a clinical garden and we are not clinical gardeners. I am strongly against the use of compounds that interfere with the balance of bird, animal and plant life. For instance, moles have been very active in the woodland this month and at one time worked uncomfortably near the lawns, but by tracing their runs and placing pieces of stem of the wild spurge inside, we turned them back.

I like to clean up the old orchards by the end of the month. Long grass at the base of the trees, a favoured place for the eggs of woolly aphis, must be cut down, and fallen apples removed to the compost heap. Birds have had their fill, friends have taken them away by the bagfull for their horses, and all that remains is a smell reminiscent of cider. Once clean, the grass soon thickens up, and the tips of daffodil leaves can emerge without fear of being trampled on.

A double row of *Chamaecyparis lawsoniana* Columnaris Glauca, running from the terrace steps to the croquet lawn, divides the main grass area. The trees had become misshapen at the top and basal growth was very sparse due mainly to wind and snow damage. Four years ago I took the drastic step of reducing them by 2m (6ft), and I know now that it was the right decision. They have thickened beyond my hopes and are making new growth at the base and top. This is not the best of land for some conifers but a winter dressing of bonemeal will encourage healthy growth and good colour.

Either side of this avenue we have a group of *Robinia pseudoacacia*, a tree well suited to this dry soil. Its fern-like foliage is attractive throughout the summer, and the deeply fissured bark colours well into winter. The older of the two groups forms an unusual feature: five closely planted trees emerge from a circular mound of earth at an angle of 20°, and from a distance give the appearance of one large tree with divided trunks. As much as I like these trees they cause a lot of work, their brittle growth continuously dropping to the lawn, especially after strong winds.

It is an ideal time, weather permitting, to continue the spreading of compost, with rose beds and herbaceous borders receiving first priority. I prefer to leave the compost on the surface for a week or two, allowing the frosts to break up the texture, before lightly forking it in. A little is kept aside for the sole purpose of enriching the subsoil below newly planted subjects.

Iron gates in stone walls and gaps in yew hedges lead to many small individual gardens, among which we have one that has been loosely named the 'Grey Garden' for the past twenty years. Grey it may have been, but a 15 metre square walled garden, dominated by a mulberry tree on one side and a huge elm on the other, is hardly the spot to grow sun-loving plants. The elm has died, as indeed they all have here, letting in a lot more light, and the mulberry was trimmed to a beter shape. I have retained some of the original shrub planting, including a large drift of *Senecio laxifolius*, *Viburnum tinus* and its variegated form, *Choisya ternata* and *Viburnum* × *burkwoodii*. *Deutzia pulchra*, *Philadelphus* Virginal, *Osmarea* × *burkwoodii* and *Aralia elata* Albomarginata give lift to the south-facing border, and on the walls we have *Lonicera* × *purpusii* with its fragrant white flowers in winter, *Hydrangea petiolaris* and the pink and white forms of *Clematis montana*. I intend to introduce many other plants to this captivating little garden – now reverted in name to the original 'Maids' Garden' – this coming spring. As a break from routine work I asked John and Stuart to make a list of plants of their own choosing, plus suggestions for improving the general design, and pooling these with my own ideas we should have the basis of an interesting new garden.

The worst of the weather is yet to come, and as a precautionary measure I am moving some young plants raised from cuttings last September to a cold frame. They are mainly varieties which are on the border line of hardiness, penstemons, hebes, *Convolvulus mauritanicus* and one or two greys More than likely the parent plant would survive a normal winter, but heavy rain and March winds can often mean casualties and I prefer to keep replacements in hand. I also have some pans of special seedlings – *Aquilegia bertolonii*, a very deeply coloured form of *Pulsatilla vulgaris*, symphyandra, alpine campanula and verbena – and although these will stand any amount of frost they do not like wet feet, so I shall remove them to a frame until April.

All viburnums grow well on limestone, and we rely on three varieties to bring a little colour to dark winter days. Perhaps the most accommodating of them all is the evergreen *Viburnum tinus*, its pink-tinted buds opening to white lacy heads of flower from October onwards, and at their best here in January. It will grow almost

Jasminum nudiflorum

27

anywhere, but I find that semi-shade and some protection from cold winds suit it admirably. We also have the golden variegated form, a tender shrub needing the shelter of a warm wall. *Viburnum fragrans* is a universal favourite, of upright habit and opening its delicously scented white flowers, often tinged pink, any time from November onwards. The bronzy foliage is attractive also. A little thought is needed, however, in positioning this viburnum to be seen at its best. An old woody specimen of ours has a background of yew, allowing us to see the small clusters of flower across the lawn on the dullest of days. Another group is tucked into a corner against a north-facing wall, and is equally free in producing flower.

Our other winter flowerer is *Viburnum* × *bodnantense* Dawn, a hybrid of later introduction having *V. fragrans* as one of its parents. It is vigorous and reliable, showing the tubular deep pink rounded clusters of flower in early January. I think it prefers a sunny position by choice and produces frost-resistant flowers over a long period.

I always look forward to the first flowers of *Jasminum nudiflorum*, so bright and cheerful. It is not the easiest of climbers to train, having a tendency to become a tangled mass unless a little time is spent on removing shoots that have flowered as well as old black wood. In the old shrubbery *Prunus subhirtella* Autumnalis continues to bear semi-double white flowers in great profusion, but top marks must go to *Acer griseum*, the paper-barked maple, for showing off orange tints under peeling bark.

Our only *Hamamelis mollis* is against the lodge wall, and though growing in the poorest of stony soil it greets us every morning with its curious spidery flowers on leafless branches. Primroses in shady corners are sending up the first of their new stems, and snowdrops are budding on the woodland banks.

Seven swans fly in daily to feed in our bottom lake, ducks and moorhens are courting, and a young sparrow hawk keeps a sharp eye on everything that moves in the woods. Could it be that they sense a continuation of the mild weather?

FEBRUARY

During the early part of the month the mild weather remained with us, giving several really warm days with fitful sun followed by sharp night frost. By any standard this is friendly gardening weather for this time of the year, allowing us to continue with many seasonal tasks including the pruning of soft fruit, cultivation of ground as winter vegetables are cleared and, perhaps the most important of all, planting of new stock. So often it arrives when planting conditions are totally unsuitable, but for once we are able to place both bare-rooted and container-grown subjects in their permanent quarters.

I like to keep the fruit cage well stocked, and although we raise our own currants and gooseberries by cuttings from selected stock it is good policy to buy in fresh certified stock every so often. Some of the old redcurrants are past their best and I am replacing them with the variety Laxton's No 1, the best type on this soil.

On account of its earliness and heavy yielding proclivities, I allow the blackberry Himalayan Giant to remain. Over-generous planting in the past has led to some difficulty in controlling the 3m (10ft) of growth that can be produced in one season, and now we are reducing the plants to three in number to make training much easier. The Oregon thornless blackberry is slightly less vigorous and of excellent flavour, but I find that it needs a rather acid soil, necessitating in our case heavy dressings annually of leafmould and compost.

On the best of the days we continue to compost flower beds and shrubberies but by the end of the third week huge dark clouds are rolling in and on the 21st we awake to a 20cm (8in) covering of snow. The countryside as always looks beautiful, but it does present problems in the garden as sheer weight of snow can cause considerable damage to some plants. Worst hit by far is the box hedging, *Buxus sempervirens*, which surrounds the rectangular beds on the formal terracing. Over 60cm (2ft) in width and ballooned at each corner, it always seems to gather the full depth of snow, and unless the weight is considerably reduced quickly it inevitably causes a series of black holes and bulging sides that take a year or more to recover. The two *Magnolia grandiflora* at the south door of the manor are also very vulnerable, as their brittle branches will not stand much weight. *Osmanthus delavayi* and *Cytisus* × *praecox* can also suffer.

As rain disperses the snow the true winter returns, and biting cold winds and severe frost put a stop to any work on the land. Viburnums continue to provide us with interest and colour. *V. bodnantense* Dawn seems to withstand anything the elements can throw at it and indeed more than deserves the Award of Merit that the RHS bestowed upon it.

Early primroses are a sheer delight, and after the snow many bulbous subjects are struggling into flower. On the rockery *Iris histrioides* Major is the first to show, a most beautiful and distinct variety with large blue flowers on 10cm (4in) stems, closely followed by the canary-yellow *I. danfordiae*. Various forms of *I. reticulata* are in bud but need a warm day to unfold, while in a sheltered pocket *Crocus ancyrensis* gives a fine display with its small but freely produced orange-yellow flowers.

In the courtyard garden sheltered by walls on three sides, *Helleborus niger* pushes up its many stems topped with pure white

Leucojum vernum

Viburnum × *bodnantense* Dawn

'roses'; other varieties that are showing signs of new growth and flower formation are *H. foetidus, H. lividus corsicus* and *H.* × *sternii.*

Our true harbinger must be the winter aconite, *Eranthis hyemalis.* Here we have huge drifts of them under trees and on grassy banks, armies of them lining the woodland paths. They are sometimes hidden by the uncut winter grass, but when the sun shines their globular buds open out to show us the brightest of yellows, a reminder of warmer days to come. They grow and increase rapidly in these surroundings, as do the thousands of snowdrops in their single and double forms. In a sheltered part of a small walled garden there are clumps of a much taller variety of snowdrop, sometimes blooming in January, with strong wide foliage and flowers of great substance. I think it could be *Galanthus atkinsii.*

In the same genus, *Amaryllidaceae,* we have the leucojum. The earliest to flower is *Leucojum vernum,* the spring snowflake, needing a warm sheltered corner to show off to best advantage the white bells each tipped with pale green dots – a truly charming little plant.

Under a three hundred year old beech tree in the Spring garden, a sea of young green leaves has suddenly appeared. They belong to *Chionodoxa luciliae, C. sardensis* and *Scilla sibirica,* and within a few days will be transformed into a blue carpet. It is a perfect setting for them, undisturbed and warm in the leafy soil, semi-shaded in the summer by a majestic tree.

The flow of water from the spring seems unusually heavy this year, bringing down silt and dead leaves. To sweep the canal clean is a good job for a rainy day; carried out three or four times a year, it prevents a build-up of weed and twigs, and greatly enhances the overall appearance of the garden throughout the year. The temperature of the water remains a constant 4°C (39°F), winter and summer alike, unexpectedly warm for a January morning but ice-cold on a midsummer day. The canal has built-in plant chambers, ideal one would have thought for water lilies, yet the cold conditions are not at all favourable for this plant.

In the greenhouse, primulas continue to be the mainstay of flowering plants, along with forms of cineraria, celsias, azaleas and the last of the autumn-sown browallias, supplying me with enough material to brighten the manor house.

An old favourite of mine is *Cineraria hybrida* Stellata, not often seen these days, producing small flowers in great profusion on branching stems well above the foliage. Easily raise from seed, it is an accommodating plant, much more suited to house conditions than its Hybrida Grandiflora counterpart. Admittedly, for sheer brilliance of

31

colour and zoning the hybrid strains are unbeatable, but they are quick to show their intolerance of central heating. Stellata needs a final pot size of at least 16cm (6¼ in) (larger if specimen plants are to be grown), regular feeding as soon as flower buds appear, as well as a sharp eye for any aphid infestation.

A batch of bulbs brought in from the frames come quickly into flower when introduced to a little extra warmth. *Scilla sibirica* Spring Beauty and the crocus varieties Remembrance and Snowstorm are excellent for this purpose; grown in pans and topped with a little green moss, they present a picture of spring on a winter's day. With a minimum of heat, *Iris reticulata* also responds well, together with the hyacinths L'Innocence (pure white), Lady Derby (pale pink) and Bismark (bright blue), filling the house with their scent.

Ever popular, young plants of *Zygocactus truncatus*, the Christmas cactus, are nicely in bud but seem reluctant to open until temperatures rise. A legacy from the past, a group of Cymbidium orchids seem none the worse after some very cold nights, perhaps only a degree or two above freezing. Apart from slight spotting on the leaves they appear in good health, most are sporting well budded flower stems and one variety has a dozen exquisite pale lemon-yellow flowers fully out. Another orchid that flowers surprisingly well is Paphiopedilum. Ours has handsome chocolate-brown and lime-green colouring, taking on almost artificial qualities.

Calceolarias are now moved on to 12.5cm (5in) pots. I see that some of the lower leaves have a touch of mildew, and careful ventilation will be needed during the next few weeks, as well as a minimum of watering.

Normally I would not contemplate any seed sowing in a cool house this month, but as we have an electrically operated warming bench in the propagating house, it is possible to make an early start with some varieties. The thermostat is set at 18°C (65°F) giving sufficient bottom heat for the successful germination of most seeds. Early tomato plants become a practical proposition, and as space is at a premium during March and April a start can be made with flower seeds to provide a wide range of pot plants for the coming year. These include *Exacum affine,* coleus, browallia Blue Troll and impatiens.

Sowings of vegetable seeds can also be made now. Lettuce Tom Thumb and cauliflower Dok Elgon are two varieties that respond well to protection in the early stages in readiness for cultivation under cloches. Sweet peas are sown in pots in the cold frame, varieties being the almond pink Mrs R. Bolton and the white Swan Lake, the two colours most asked for.

Through choice we make up our own seed-sowing and potting soils, the ingredients being sterilised loam, peat, sand and grit, to which lime and fertiliser are added as necessary. Like many other head gardeners I have my own formulas, the mixtures varying according to the likes or dislikes of individual plants. They key factor of course, is the quality of the loam: it must be fibrous and from the top spit, for without this compost can become thin and lifeless. I regret to say that the majority of composts sold to the public nowadays are of poor quality and would strongly advise any keen gardener who can maintain a loam stack to make up his own mixture.

This month is a good time to give a little attention to standard and bush fuchsias. They should be knocked out from their pots and as much old soil as possible carefully removed before they are re-potted in slightly smaller pots. A daily syringing with tepid water will soon encourage them into growth, and they can then be pruned hard back to produce strong new shoots suitable for growing on or as propagating material.

Just how long the kitchen garden has been used as such is a matter for speculation; a hundred years for certainty and probably a further hundred as well. A stone plaque set in the wall near a multi-espaliered Pitmaston Duchess pear of great age reads: 'Near this stone was buried the agreeable and excellent little spaniel Flint. She died October 27.1784, more friendly & faithful creature never existed.'

In keeping with my policy to return to the land as much as is taken out in the course of a season, every morsel of organic material is composted and turned into a source of rich humus. Vegetable waste, grass cuttings, young annual weeds and coarse plant stems are all used, and along with bins of maturing leafmould plus the winter stockpile of strawy horse manure this compost enables me to build up and maintain soil fertility.

Schools of thought on gardening differ greatly, and generations of head gardeners can be divided into organic or inorganic thinkers. In many cases the fertility of the soil has been allowed to drain away. I personally like few paths in a kitchen garden; when I took over here they were so numerous that at first glance it resembled a research establishment. All was soon put to rights, enabling us to grow long straight rows of vegetables across the garden, but evidently some form of toxic weedkiller was used on the old paths which, to this day, has a slight retarding effect on growing crops.

Apart from heavy dressings of manure and compost I like to rest

Part of the kitchen garden in February, showing ryegrass strips

one eighth of the total area every year. To leave the ground fallow, especially during winter, allows heavy rains to leach away valuable plant foods. Italian ryegrass sown in September at the rate of 15g (½oz) to the square metre will all but stop this, at the same time providing fibre to a thin soil as well as valuable minerals drawn up through the roots.

At the end of the month I shall ask Norman to dig in half the grass area and by early spring it should break down to a fibrous tilth for peas, beans and sweet corn. The remainder is allowed to grow and thicken all summer with an occasional cut to prevent it running to seed, then dug in during early autumn for winter vegetables.

Although I am constantly trying to improve the fertility of the land its very shallowness over limestone can often lead to deficiencies in plant growth. On a neutral to alkaline soil vegetables will seldom, if ever, suffer from a lack of calcium, but a magnesium deficiency is more common than is generally realised, being quickly identified by chlorosis of the leaf. The centres of leaves become pale followed by tissue damage along the midrib. The lack of certain elements show a distinct pattern of chlorosis, but only by very careful observation and experience can one pinpoint a deficiency by this method.

Soft fruit, particularly raspberries, are quick to show a want of magnesium in early summer, often after heavy rain. It is fortunate

34

that corrective measures are easy and quick to carry out by an application of magnesium sulphate.

Having completed the pruning of all soft fruit by the middle of the month it is now time to give them a top dressing of fertiliser. The individual needs of different fruits are complex, but potash is one element that must be well represented to produce the quality. Tomato fertilisers are excellent, or a general one with added potash. Don't forget the established apples and pears – all will greatly improve in growth and production by a top dressing this month.

About now we tip our raspberries, cutting them back to 7.5cm (3in) above the top supporting wire. This task must be completed before early March to avoid bleeding from the rising sap. Autumn fruiting varieties are cut down to the ground and canes growing away from the rows carefully dug out. What a valuable addition to any garden these late raspberries are, bearing fruit on the current season's growth for many weeks. The variety we grow is September, living up to its name by producing excellent quality fruit in autumn, sometimes into November. I allow the new canes to grow freely without tying in, the only support being a single wire placed either side of the row in August to encourage stems to arch over, thus giving the maximum circulation of air to discourage mildew.

Alongside one of the grass paths we grow a long row of the alpine strawberry Delices. The top leaves are left on all winter as a form of protection, but now they are cut away, the crowns cleaned up and some general fertiliser worked in around the root area. There are numerous varieties to choose from – Baron Solemacher has a fine flavour – but by and large I find Delices a reliable and heavy cropper. Fresh plants are raised from seed every three years, by far the best method to keep young healthy stock. They can suffer from moisture loss in a dry summer, appreciating some form of irrigation at this time to keep the fruit firm and juicy. An accommodating and trouble-free crop, these strawberries are always in demand during the summer for dinner parties and such, they make excellent jam, freeze well, and personally I adore them for breakfast. To pick a punnet or two on a summer's evening is, to me, great joy.

Once again it is time to order seed potatoes, the accent being on quality more than quantity, although in some cases it is possible to combine the two merits. By trial and error we now know the varieties that are suited to our land: Pentland Javelin, Sutton's Foremost and Maris Bard for earlies, Désirée and Majestic for the maincrop. As seed becomes available they are trayed out in the apple house, which is cool but frost free, and allowed to develop sturdy chits before being planted. John is very keen on growing some of the old varieties that are still available in small quantities from specialist growers. Basically I am only interested in those that grow and crop well here, but in all fairness to John I agreed to put some of his rarities to the test this summer, the results of which will be found in a later chapter.

After the first snow followed by hard frost, the land is cold to the touch and wet underfoot. I have never advocated early sowing of vegetables in this part of the country, even in a walled garden such as ours. Soil texture will just not allow traffic, human or mechanical, on its surface until drying winds arrive, and no seed will germinate in the cold stickiness. Being something of an optimist where vegetables are concerned, I lined out two 18m (60ft) rows with barn cloches, hoping for some early March sunshine to warm the soil beneath them. I have a feeling that it may be a late sowing season, and we may even have to wait until April before the land crumbles to a tilth.

Lettuce Tom Thumb raised under glass earlier in the month have been pricked out, forty to a tray, and placed in the cold frame to keep them hard and sturdy. Early cauliflower seedlings are potted individually into 7.5cm (3in) pots; they seem to resent root disturbance when the soil is only partially warmed, and these will grow away unchecked when planted under cloches. They too, will spend some time in the frames, being fully protected in only the severest of weather.

Normally I would sow the first row of parsnips this month as well as further broad beans, but not so this year. Checking up on the stored onions I find that a small percentage have suffered from basal rot, but generally speaking they are keeping well, especially the quality seed-raised varieties. Apples have fared even better: Cox's Orange Pippin are still firm skinned, Bramley Seedling and Howgate Wonder look as good as the day they were picked. Both apples and onions are spaced out on slatted trays sliding on the runners to form blocks ten high. Perhaps not the ideal storage method, yet they will provide for the kitchen at least until June.

The last of the celeriac roots stored in boxes of dry sand are quickly used up for soups, the few remaining sound swedes are also brought in. It is in the winter months that the previous season's surplus tomatoes, puréed into pint bags and placed in the freezer, are appreciated to the full, again making delicious soup.

There is nothing quite like fresh vegetables, but there are also warmer jobs than picking them this time of the year. Peer Gynt and Ladora continue to provide us with baskets of small firm sprouts, the last of the January King cabbage has been cut, but Celtic will stand for a number of weeks yet. I think parsnips roasted round the Sunday joint is one of the delights of winter. The variety I grew this year was Tender and True, making medium-sized clean roots. During the last month the maincrop leeks have thickened up well; we can never have too many as they are in constant demand for a great variety of dishes. Most of the early Autumn Mammoth have been dug and we now rely on Winter Reuzen, a fine quality variety with medium-sized thick stems. Regrettably, the last of the carrots have been used, but a few winter-hardy spring onions give a bite to a salad. Some roots of parsley potted in December and brought under glass are making fresh sprigs. Sprouting broccoli and spring cauliflowers are laid low by sharp frost, only to recover as days become warmer. A new season is about to start, but we must wait.

MARCH

This is a month that needs approaching with a good deal of caution
the odd sunny day can so easily be interpreted as a herald of spring.
We know only too well that in the Cotswolds it is a month renowned
for snow showers and biting winds, and the professional gardener
can feel it as one of the coldest of the year.

This year is no exception, and with the addition of abnormally
heavy rainfall the growing season will have a slow start.
Unfortunately, a vast amount of work presents itself about now, but
as yet it is a case of selecting certain tasks to fit in with the weather.
We can wait, but nature, unlike us, is impatient and the garden is
coming to life. Many bulbous subjects are pushing their way
through to the surface, trees and shrubs unfold new foliage, lawns
have lost their winter greyness to become green again.

The aconites and snowdrops are slowly fading as we look forward
to a succession of spring flowers. *Iris histrioides* Major now has to
contend with a crust of snow, which accentuates its beauty and slight
scent. Dotted about the rock garden and along the terrace walls we
have plantings of *I. reticulata*, its violet-purple heads with a golden
blotch never failing to catch the eye. As well as the type, we grow
one or two of its delightful hybrids: the pale blue Cantab is a
charmer and follows the early reddish-purple J. S. Dijt. Where the
soil is stony they have naturalised well, and as long as they receive a
period of sun-ripening they will continue to flower freely each year. I
cannot say the same for *I. danfordiae* whose numbers dwindle
annually. I have a particular liking for this bright little species, and
while it remains relatively cheap to buy I shall continue to plant and
admire it. Both slugs and great tits can cause havoc among them,
but they are surely worth protecting.

Asking for very little, but giving great pleasure, is *Anemone blanda.*
These anemones pop up everywhere here, under shrubs and
through carpeting thymes, edging formal beds and in the rock
garden, and although they seed profusely they are never a nuisance.
Aptly named the Grecian windflower and blooming for several

Soldanella carpatica in a stone trough. A harbinger of spring, this true alpine appreciates some protection from heavy winter rains

Early crocuses surround a group of false acacias

Anemone blanda

weeks, their colours range from white to deep red. Possibly the best variety is *A. b. atrocoerulea* with its intense blue flowers.

Chionodoxas, scillas and tritelias by the thousand are in flower in the Spring garden, a truly marvellous sight. The raised grass mound surrounding a group of false acacias on the main lawn is home for many crocuses, the first to flower being *Crocus tomasinianus* in pale and deep coloured forms. The pale forms are almost grey in bud until a brighter day opens them up to show off their amethyst blue petals. The interior shading of deep lilac in the variety Barr's Purple is also very colourful. *C. chrysanthus* in its hybrid forms are well worth growing: Snowbunting, E. P. Bowles and Princess Beatrix are a few varieties, all producing small flowers in great abundance. For sheer quantity of bloom, *C. ancyrensis* must win hands down – what a picture they are along the base of a yew hedge. *C. sieberi* Violet Queen has perhaps all the qualities I look for in a crocus: a great profusion of flower and a startling contrast between deep orange anthers and satin purple petals.

The large-flowered forms come in with a rush, yellows being traditionally the first followed by white and striped, and then blue and purple shades. Many of these I have planted in the last five years, some where giant elms once stood, others beneath the weeping pears that line the canal, amongst shrubs, and down the main drive. I can never have too many, and there is room for thousands more. Squirrels take a great liking to the corms, and I gather that some years ago they completely annihilated the drive plantings. A visiting Dutch grower suggested planting *Fritillaria imperialis* (crown imperial) as a deterrent, and from that day on both squirrels and mice have kept their distance in this area. The last crocus to flower is The Bishop, the deepest purple I have seen with a beautiful velvet sheen.

Following the irises in the rock garden are groups of cyclamineus narcissus hybrids, March Sunshine being the first to flower. What a lovely name for this slightly reflexed deep yellow variety, and those that follow have equally attractive names: Peeping Tom, Tête-à-Tête and Dove Wings. Their earliness and highly individual reflexed forms make these narcissi indispensable for March colour. The dwarf *N. W. P. Milner* has been extensively planted in the rock garden area, probably before its price rocketed, for who can afford to buy it in quantity now? Even so, the lemon yellow trumpets on 20cm (8in) stems stand up to any weather. The most dwarf of all is *N. minimus* with perfect little daffodils only 7.5cm (3in) high. It is the only small species that will grow and increase in our soil. Others I have tried with little success; perhaps they need an acid or moisture-retentive pocket.

Adjacent to the rock garden is an informal bed, again due to the death of an elm. Here I have planted some interesting conifers and a number of *Erica carnea*, along with *Campanula lactiflora, Hypericum*

Narcissus Tête-à-Tête, an enchanting free flowering cyclamineus hybrid growing only 15cm (6in) high

Hidcote var, agapanthus and bergenia. Showing to their best advantage against the leathery leaves of bergenia are clumps of *Muscari botryoides* Album, the early and also scented white grape hyacinth. Some tulip species grow well here, including *Tulipa eichleri* with scarlet bell-shaped flowers, the pointed petals rising from a black base, all of which are set off by attractive metallic foliage. Only 10cm (4in) high, *T. biflora* has small clusters of cream flowers, while *T. turkestanica* is slightly taller with up to nine pure white flowers on the one stem. The petals carry a green flush, making this an interesting and worthwhile addition.

The water-lily tulip, *T. kaufmanniana* is a long lived and charming species, equally at home on the rockery or in the border. It has also produced a number of extremely colourful hybrids which need only shelter from the wind. Two varieties I grow and am vey fond of are The First, which really is first, with white cups coloured red on the exterior, and Shakespeare with multi-coloured shading, predominantly apricot.

The primrose, and to a lesser degree, the polyanthus are normally associated with the country garden, yet when I first came to Cornwell there were none to be seen except for a few wild primroses in the orchards. Although valuable as an edging, it is 'en masse' that the true beauty of these spring flowers can be fully appreciated. Looking for a suitable site led me to an island bed in the lower lawn shaded by tall yew and sycamore. Originally planted with a selection of philadelphus, the bed had been allowed to run wild, with ground elder and thistle taking over. A year's persistent forking gave me an ideal site; the philadelphus were drastically reduced and are now pruned annually to provide shade only. The soil was extremely shallow, almost as if the top spit had been removed, (perhaps it had), so that heavy dressings of leafmould and once-used greenhouse soil were required. During that year I raised over one hundred plants of the Biedermeier Strain primrose, resulting in many colourful forms but rather too many orange and red shades. Since then, by using seed from a specialist grower, I have increased the range with unusual pastel shades, including some delightful pinks, lemon- and orange-yellows, russets and a whole range of blues. To these I have added Juliana polyanthus, the bronze-leaved Cowichan polyanthus that are self coloured with golden eyelets, and plants from double primrose seed that produced seven fully double forms. Also included in this bed are polygonum, dicentra, alchemilla (lady's mantle) and campanula, all contributing to what is normally a very colourful part of the garden in April.

Not by any stretch of the imagination can this be classed as an early garden – far from it; but I am always interested in winter flowering plants as long as they are completely hardy and weather resistant. Hellebores come into this category; although their flowers can be badly pitted by heavy rain they are robust enough to warrant numerous places in the garden. The native plant, *Helleborus foetidus* has been grown here for some years, and to this I have added *H. lividus corsicus* with its extremely handsome trifoliate leaves and panicles of apple green flowers. *H.* × *sternii* is a hybrid of the former with variable lime-green colourings. Some *H. orientalis* have been raised from seed, mainly of the spotted type on white or maroon-purple backgrounds, and I look forward to seeing them bloom. *Helleborus* Anderson's Red is also a good deep claret shade, associating well with chionodoxas and tritelias. On a north-facing wall or hedge they form unexpected patches of winter colour, and most grow well on chalk with a regular mulch of leaf-mould.

Up to within a few years ago I could never raise much enthusiasm for euphorbias, but now I am growing several species in my own garden as a prelude to introducing them. These spurges are invaluable as focal specimens, especially *Euphorbia wulfenii* with its

Helleborus lividus corsicus

43

glaucous foliage up to 1.2m (4ft) high and huge heads of lime-green flowers. Rather similar but not so tall is *E. characias*, whose green flowers have maroon eyes. Most euphorbias will need careful placing, as I find they easily snap in strong winds; even so, they are striking and unusual plants, worthy of a place where the soil is not too rich.

A stone trough is devoted entirely to Kabschia saxifrages, their hard mounds of silver foliage literally covered with delightful flowers in many shades. During March they are at their best: *Saxifraga burseriana* Gloria, *S. b.* Sulphurea, *S.* × *jenkinsae* and *S.* × *elizabethae* are just a few of these little gems, better in troughs or raised beds of very gritty soil than in the open garden.

We have many cherries here, the most rewarding and beautiful of our spring flowering trees, clothing their branches in a profusion of blossom seemingly unaffected by March weather. Our well-drained, limy soil is much to their liking, and from now until the end of April there is a succession of flower from horizontal, spreading and upright varieties, from the early small-flowered wild cherry to the large double Japanese kinds. The earliest is a fine specimen of *Prunus sargentii* with single pink flowers; the foliage of this cherry is brilliant

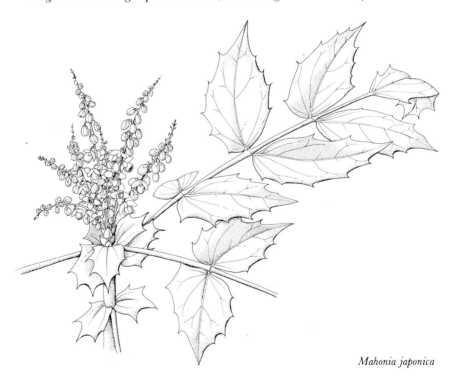

Mahonia japonica

Catkin-like racemes of the March-flowering *Corylopsis spicata*

red in the autumn. Seeing it on the lodge lawn with a background of *Forsythia suspensa fortunei*, hyacinths and early narcissus, against an expanse of Cotswold stone wall, who could fail to stop and admire?

Viburnums continue to flower but sparsely now. The weight of blossom has faded, as is the case with the autumn cherry, *Prunus subhirtella* Autumnalis and its pink form Rosea.

On the south wall of the manor there is that very choice shrub, *Mahonia japonica*. Its long racemes of yellow flowers are with us for most of the winter and the large pinnate leaves are attractive all the year round. Preferring some shade, it will remain happy in full sun, as it is here, as long as the root system does not dry out during summer.

Round the corner on the east wall, the cydonia *Chaenomeles* Simonii, a quince of great merit, clothes its leafless stems with deep red blooms. At the main gate the silky catkins of an old *Salix caprea* are a fine sight. It is more of a rambling shrub than a tree, with broad grey-green leaves, and the conspicuous yellow anthers are much visited by insects on a warm day. The dwarf willows are all interesting, varying greatly in habit and catkin formation: *S. Wehrhahnii* is a sturdy grower with large white catkins and polished stems, *S. helvetica* seldom exceeds 60cm (2ft) in height, with lemon catkins and almost round silvery leaves. We also grow *S. lanata*

45

stuartii which has spectacular catkins and silver-grey leaves. In the rock garden *S. apoda*, *S. polaris* and *S. repens argentea* are useful forms, the latter needing plenty of room but making a glorious picture as it tumbles over a tall stone.

If I had to choose one favourite shrub for March it would have to be *Corylopsis spicata*; its simple beauty outshines any other. The fragrant flowers are borne as catkin-like racemes up to 15cm (6in) long, well spaced apart. It must have protection from cold winds and early morning spring frosts, conditions we can provide against a west wall, tucked in between *Prunus* Kanzan and *Viburnum opulus*. Though not a lime-lover it will grow in a neutral soil, and here it seems to benefit by an overflow of rainwater from a narrow guttering.

The pruning of hybrid tea and floribunda roses must be completed by the end of the month. It is also the ideal time for dividing herbaceous plants where clumps are too large or woody.

As outside work is well up to schedule, or in some cases temporarily halted because of weather conditions, I am able to turn my attention to work under glass. It is a mixed blessing perhaps when the rain drives us inside, for this month is an extremely busy one in the propagating and plant house. The routine chores of pot-washing, soil-mixing and general glasshouse hygiene earlier in the year can now be fully appreciated.

Most gardeners, I'm sure, have their special likes and dislikes where tomatoes are concerned, and I am no exception. Flavour and texture must be of prime importance, size and weight secondary, yet nowadays it is not so easy to find these qualities. I well remember twenty-five years ago, when I first started to take tomato growing seriously, varieties such as Ailsa Craig, Plumpton King, Money-maker and Harbinger could be relied upon to produce disease-free plants and abundant quality fruit. Most are still available, and during the last five years I have once again grown a small batch of these old faithfuls, only to be disappointed in the resulting crop. Perhaps – and this is only my opinion – the selection of tomatoes for seed purposes has not been rigorously controlled, for now virus disease and the unpopular 'greenback' are all too common. Great strides have been made to eliminate this with the introduction of FI hybrids, but as many of these require specialised growing conditions a careful choice must be made. This year I am growing three sorts, Alicante, FI Hybrid MM and Tangella. The first two provide well flavoured, quality fruit, and the third is always being asked for by the kitchen on account of its mild flavour and orange skin, so popular as a decorative addition. Most important of all, they are suited to cool house temperatures. Sowings are made in two batches, end of February and mid-March. Seed compost is brought in and warmed for a couple of days – most important – before filling up some well crocked seed pans. Germination is even and rapid over a bottom heat of 15°C (60°F), and it is now that the maximum light, obtained through glass that is clean inside and out, is so necessary to keep seedlings short and sturdy.

Zonal and ivy-leaved pelargoniums, raised from cuttings last September and potted into 7.5cm (3in) pots during October, seem none the worse for our lower minimum temperature during the winter. They are fast making new growth, pots are well filled with roots, and during the next few days we shall pot them on into 12.5cm (5in) pots using a mixture similar to John Innes No 2.

Although day temperatures can rise quite dramatically now, the night temperatures can fall to the minimum, and it is important that watering is carefully controlled. This applies in general to all growing plants under glass during March; a pot full of cold wet soil is a sure killer.

Show pelargoniums, also raised from cuttings last August, have not fared quite so well, this branch of the family liking a few extra degrees of warmth. However, after losses we still have sufficient sturdy plants to meet our requirements, and these too are making new leaves and will need potting on by the middle of the month. I find they respond well to a fibrous mixture, and for this we use six parts loam, four parts peat and two parts sand by bulk. All growth is kept well pinched back until mid-April, forming tight clumps of basal shoots.

Begonia and gloxinia corms now need some attention, having spent the winter in their original pots, perfectly dry under the staging. Old stems and roots are carefully rubbed off and the corms inspected for any signs of decay or mould. They are then placed in seed trays with a mixture of two parts sand and one part peat, with their tops just showing, after which a little bottom heat will soon induce them into growth.

One of the most brilliant bulbous plants is the amaryllis (*Hippeastrum*). Re-potting is not necessary every year – in fact they resent it – but by removing some of the old soil, soaking the dry roots in tepid water and topping up with fresh compost, the plants' needs are catered for. Potting must be firm, after which they are stood in the warmest part of the house, watering being kept on the lean side until flower stems appear.

Fragrance is such an important attribute under glass, and what better subjects than lilies to provide it. Space alone prevents me from growing masses of them, but room I can find for *Lilium regale* and its yellow counterpart Royal Gold. Some hybrids are also excellent for pot culture, Fire King and Enchantment being two I particularly like. Bulbs should be purchased as early as possible in the new year and planted three to a 20cm (8in) pot. Soil needs to be well drained with the addition of leafmould and well rotted manure. Most lilies are stem rooting, so allow sufficient room for topping up. The cold frame is the best place for them until growth is well advanced and roots are curling round the pot.

Acidanthera bicolor murieliae is seldom seen as a cool house plant, but it is deliciously fragrant. A dozen bulbs in a large pot make a wonderful display. I wonder why achimenes are not more popular, for here is a fairly easy and free-flowering plant that all cool house owners should grow. Over the years I have built up a collection of very colourful varieties; they increase rapidly and are tolerant of indoor treatment. Having spent the winter undisturbed beneath the benching, they are now knocked out of their pots and the small rhizomes carefully removed from the base of the old stem. Placed in sandy soil and just covered, they soon form new shoots. Alternatively they can be planted in their flowering pots about 2cm (¾ in) deep – five to a 15cm (6in) pot is ideal. I prefer to transplant them, but it is a matter of choice. Note, however, that if bottom heat is not available, they should be left alone until April. Smithianthas need exactly the same treatment, but their caterpillar-like rhizomes are brittle and need careful handling. Other bulbous subjects that require some form of re-potting include eucomis, haemanthus (blood lily), ismenes and nerines.

Primulas and cinerarias continue to be the main supply of pot plants; *Azalea indica*, too, is now full of flower. The first of the freesias raised from seed last June fill the house with their strong scent. Tall subjects are always in demand for decorating the large hall and staircase, and for this I have to rely on *Jasminum primulinum* grown as a weeping standard. It is rarely seen in this form, its long trailing branches covered with semi-double fragrant yellow flowers. Almost hardy and needing protection only in the coldest of months, it is easily raised from cuttings and trained to a standard in about two years. The plants need large pots and a lot of space, and fortunately we have both.

Clivia miniata is showing numerous fat heads of bud, so watering and feeding will now be increased. What room is left on the heated bench is taken up with pans of seed. As we have over thirty tubs and urns to fill with summer flowers, sowings of cascade petunias and trailing lobelia are made now. I have reduced bedding out to one

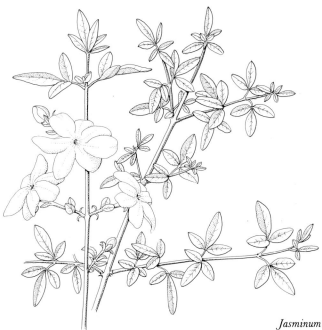

Jasminum primulinum

circular area below an *Acer negundo* Variegatum in the pool garden.
This year I shall use dianthus Magic Charms, which I hope will be
as colourful as last season's verbena. Also raised this month are
Hypoestes sanguinolenta, Torenia fournieri and the solanum Red Giant,
and for the kitchen garden, celery, celeriac and early summer
cabbage.

Any thoughts of bringing the land in the kitchen garden to a tilth are
dashed as rain continues to fall most days. Frost we can tolerate,
cold winds we can turn our back on, but heavy rain this month
brings only frustration and strong language.

As the ground is cleared of winter cabbage and sprouts, it is
composted and dug over, a muddy job that nobody relishes, yet
important if any benefit is to be gained from frost and wind. The
autumn-sown ryegrass is nearly 30cm (1ft) high and will need a cut
before it is turned in. This is one job that can be done in almost any
weather, slicing the ground like chocolate with a sharp spade and
completely reversing the top spit to expose a mass of fibrous roots.
Left to settle for a week or two, the ground will support some fine
rows of peas and beans. The sweet pea trench is taken out where
ryegrass has grown. 'Always use rested ground for sweet peas,' a
famous grower once told me, and I have done so ever since. Not that

49

Norman turning in ryegrass in early spring as a preparation for peas and beans

we grow them for exhibition, just a few for cutting, but the resulting vigour and the strong-stemmed blooms speak for themselves. A trench is marked out 60cm (2ft) wide and a spade's depth of soil taken out. Plenty of well rotted manure is worked into the next layer, the soil is then replaced and a good general fertiliser applied to the top 7.5cm (3in) and allowed to settle before 'sticking'.

At last we have the first picking of purple sprouting broccoli. Even fresh sprouts and leeks are temporarily forgotten when this delicious vegetable is in season. Also excellent for freezing, it requires picking every other day. Soon to be followed by the white sprouting type, which I personally find even tastier, purple sprouting broccoli provides a most welcome change for the kitchen. We do not freeze any brussels sprouts – there is seldom any room – because the picking season is spread over at least four months, and at other times of the year there are plenty of other fresh vegetables. I think one of the great joys of a kitchen garden is to look forward to the produce that each season brings.

Winter Reuzen leeks are standing well with perhaps just a little coarseness coming to some stems; even so the worst will make marvellous soup. Good firm cabbage can now be produced almost all the year round, and it is a relatively easy task to control maturity times from June to December. Once the old faithful January King has finished it is not so easy. Recent years have seen the introduction of several winter varieties boasting cutting dates as late as April, but our experience with them has proved otherwise, many cabbages maturing around Christmas and some ruined by frost. A variety that is winter hardy is Celtic, perhaps because it has some savoy in its breeding. We also grow Hidena, a late Dutch type that will lift and store well if extreme weather is imminent.

Sadly, we have dug the last of the parsnips, strangely enough at a time when we are waiting to sow fresh seed. Some winter cauliflowers are showing signs of heading up, and to help them through this spell of unkind weather we cover a few of the more advanced with barn cloches. Timing is so important in producing heads from late March until May that only by trial and error can one compile a list of varieties that will do just this. Saint David No 3, April Queen and Walcheren will normally cover this period on our land. As a gamble I have grown a few plants of Snow's Winter White with a view to cutting in January and February. In a mild winter they are successful, but four times out of five they succumb to the Cotswold climate.

We have a large number of barn cloches of the Chase type and an even larger amount of cloche fittings needing glass, now an expensive commodity. I still much prefer them to the modern plastic types, which can be whisked away by strong winds unless firmly anchored. The one big advantage of the barn cloche is the high sides allowing full development as well as maximum light and air circulation. A row placed across the garden at the end of last month has warmed and partly dried the soil below, giving ideal conditions to receive young plants of lettuce Tom Thumb from the frames. These are small compact lettuces that can be planted 30cm (1ft) apart, in our case in a double staggered row, without crowding them. Early carrots are also successful under cloches, but only if the soil warmth can be maintained. However, it is so easy to overdo early planting of vegetables, resulting in poor germination and hard stunted growth. I prefer to bide my time, as so often seeds sown later in a warm soil will catch up and outgrow those under protection.

Two fine days gave us the opportunity to plant the first of the maincrop broad beans. Soil preparation is not so vital for this crop – a five-pronged cultivator drawn through to aerate the surface of well dug ground is all that is necessary. Seeds are sown individually with the trowel, and footmarks are loosened up to prevent panning. Both the white- and green-seeded varieties are delicious when picked young. For protected cultivation The Sutton is a more suitable variety than most, and for freezing purposes I would choose a green-seeded type, as these seem to retain their flavour over a longer period.

Rhubarb crowns are showing signs of life, and by placing one of our old 30cm (12in) clay pots over them we are assured of a few fresh sticks by the end of the month. The early variety is Early Albert, suitable for limited forcing but rather lacking in flavour. The bright red stems of Cawood Castle are far superior in every way although not so freely produced.

In the country a heavy distribution of annual weed seed is inevitable; the problem is that they seem to lack any close season for germination. I well remember the day when groundsel and speedwell were blackened by sharp frost, but now they seem immune and grow through the winter. It is essential, even this early in the season, that some control is carried out to prevent these weeds seeding.

Good pea sticks we can never have too many of, and as hazel coppices are few in number on the estate we cut sparingly. Well feathered young whips, 1.2–1.5m (4–5ft) high, are ideal for peas, with a few taller ones for sweet peas. They last us for two summers, and by laying in fresh bundles every year a plentiful stock is maintained.

Generally speaking, large estates and country houses have reduced their area of kitchen garden. In many instances, for economic reasons, they have been discontinued. I am constantly aware and proud of the fact that we are able to maintain ours to a high standard and incorporate its unique design and setting into the complete picture.

APRIL

The cold grey weather persisted for a short while longer, and then at last the wind swung to the south bringing warm drying days. Lawns must have first priority, for with a wet March they have grown lush and thick. Top debris from the robinias and limes is gathered up and wormcasts brushed away with a besom. The main areas of cylinder-mown grass are rolled with a quarter-ton roller pulled behind a Wheelhorse tractor, but the terraces and small walled gardens with numerous steps present a few problems. There is only one solution: with considerable dexterity the roller is manhandled. Preparatory work such as the removal of stones picked up by muddy boots is vitally important to ensure an even cut and minimal damage to the mower. Several cuts in the next few weeks, with successive lowering of the blades, will restore the lawns to a feature that reflects the remainder of the garden.

It is a comforting thought that Stuart really enjoys grass cutting; throughout the summer he takes great pride in the upkeep and appearance of all the lawns, and due credit to him.

April is the month of the daffodil, many thousands of which are naturalised in the woodlands, by the lakeside and in the old orchards. Most were planted over twenty years ago and have since increased and flourished in this ideal environment. Varieties are those that essentially naturalise well, such as Flower Carpet, Magnificence, Fortune and Sempre Avanti to name a few, and great drifts of *Narcissus poeticus* Actaea, with its small red eye set in a pure white perianth, last well into May.

Under the National Gardens Scheme our garden is open on Easter Sunday afternoon. In recent years we have been lucky with the weather and normally we can expect over a thousand people. For a large number it is an annual visit to enjoy the woodland walks and the tranquillity of the lakes. Trees and spring bulbs provide interest, and the primroses, now in full flower, are also greatly admired.

The continuing dry weather has enabled us to start the overdue work on the herbaceous borders. Old stems and foliage are trimmed

Juliana primroses in the north facing border of the Maids' Garden. The door leads to a children's play area and the ballroom beyond

Blossom weighs down the branches of *Prunus* Shirofugen on the lodge lawn

right back to let in maximum light and air, large clumps of achillea, sedum and michaelmas daisy are divided and the best outer growth replanted. A top dressing of fertiliser is very beneficial applied now, as herbaceous plants are vigorous and quickly exhaust the food supply. Some fine, very well rotted compost is put aside for the herbaceous borders every year, and this is now spread to act as a soil conditioner and moisture conserving mulch.

Even the most carefully designed border on paper seldom lives up to expectations of colour and height control, whereas in some instances some of my more random plantings have produced a very pleasing effect. At least once a year I try to make a note of colour and form combinations that often succeed purely by chance, for once they fade they are quickly forgotten if not recorded.

Many varieties of cherry are now in flower, single and double forms, small leaved and broad leaved, they all give a profusion of blossom without fuss. *Prunus* Kanzan is probably more widely planted than any other cherry. It is undeniably beautiful in flower, yet its vigour and ultimate size can cause problems in the smaller garden. Japanese forms are so varied in colour and shape that it is possible to choose one that will adapt itself to any position, no matter how large or small. *P.* Shirofugen is spectacular in blossom, the almost horizontal branches clothed with many-petalled white flowers that turn pink before they fall. *P.* Jo-Nioi is more upright and the single white flowers are scented. We have many others, none more colourful than *P.* Kiku-shidare Sakura, or Cheal's weeping cherry, a small sturdy tree with drooping branches that curve gracefully to the ground. Four of these trees are planted at the side of the canal where the water cascades from a tunnel, and when the thick clusters of double pink flowers are fully open it is a fine sight.

A native of this country, *Fritillaria meleagris*, blooms in the semi-shade of a wall, where the bells of chequered rose and purple, and my favourite white form, are quietly charming. In contrast a row of seventy or so *F. imperialis*, the crown imperial, stands stately along the shady side of the main drive. This is certainly a handsome plant not so often seen as it used to be, and though its strong garlicky smell may be off-putting to some, I have a great liking for the way it displays the circle of orange or yellow bells. Some form of support is necessary but is soon hidden by the grassy foliage. (imperials are silhouetted against evergreens and your *Prunus cerasifera* Pissardii, and arouse great interest on (

The lure of the primrose is universal, and our infor under groups of philadelphus is photographed more th feature during spring. This bed, situated fairly low a

The white form of *Fritillaria meleagris*, requiring semi-shade and a moist root run to naturalise well

Fritillaria imperialis (crown imperial) along the main drive. ...ately appearance always ...nterest

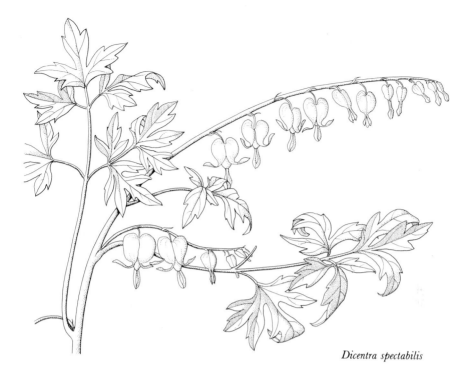

Dicentra spectabilis

the influence of nearby running water, provides an ideal home for *Dicentra spectabilis*, whose old name of 'lady's locket' aptly describes the pendant stems of heart-shaped flowers which are freely produced when this very praiseworthy plant is established. Also enjoying the cool conditions is *D. eximea*, a great weed-suffocater and ground-coverer, as is its neighbour *Polygonum bistorta* Superbum, whose invasive habit is forgotten temporarily when it produces its soft pink spikes at the end of the month.

Facing south against the manor wall, *Osmanthus delavayi* fills the air with its strong sweet fragrance; not the easiest of shrubs to establish, it is worthy of its place for the daphne-like blossom. Space commits us to clipping it each year which seems to be to its liking, sheer volume of flower almost covering the small shiny leaves.

One of its progeny, *Osmarea burkwoodii* is undoubtedly one of the finest evergreen shrubs for limestone, absolutely hardy and generous with clusters of fragrant white flowers.

The succession of early flowering viburnums is continued with *Viburnum* × *burkwoodii*. I can forgive this shrub its rangy open habit when the clusters of white flowers, pink in bud, appear, its fragrance also attracting many insects. Up by the old park gates two *V. carlesii* never fail to stop passers-by with their heavy scented flowers; the neat growth and deep pink buds put this variety in the forefront of

Osmanthus delavayi

best garden shrubs. One of its hybrids, *V. carlcephalum*, is a strong grower carrying large heads of creamy flowers but lacks the finesse of its parent. Even so I shall always grow it for its ability to flower in a bleak month.

I should dearly love to be able to grow *Narcissus cyclamineus* and *N. bulbocodium* varieties successfully, but our limy soil, which can dry so rapidly in late spring, is not very accommodating. *N. triandrus albus*, however, produces its 'Angels Tears' in great abundance. Easier by far are the tulip species, *Tulipa chrysantha* being one of the most desirable for its yellow and red cups on 15cm (6in) stems. *T. batalinii* is ideally suited for the rock garden with its beautifully formed primrose yellow flowers on only 10cm (4in) stems. The *T. greigii* hybrids are among the most colourful obtainable, for not only are the flowers delicately marked, the foliage is also attractive with mottled or striped appearance. Their short strong stems will cope with April showers, and when the sun shines the flowers open fully. Red Riding Hood and Donna Bella are two we grow, but Corsage is without doubt one of the best, its unique colour combination of bronze-apricot and yellow being further enhanced by interior feathering.

At the head of the rock garden *Anemone blanda* continues in its long season of flowering and is joined by *A. appenina*. The sky-blue

58

Pulsatilla vulgaris Rubra, a selected claret coloured form of the pasqueflower. The silky seed heads that follow are also very attractive

flowers enjoy shade, and this lovely little plant will naturalise well in cool leafy soil.

The pasqueflower, *Pulsatilla vulgaris*, unfurls feathery leaves to make way for the silky buds. It is a native of chalky downs and ideally suited to our land. Both the species and its various forms are great favourites of mine and from seed, sown as soon as it ripens, I have raised some interesting colour variations. There are several claret-red forms in cultivation, as well as the lovely *P. v.* Alba Superba with broad overlapping white petals.

A moist pocket below the first waterfall produces just the right conditions for erythronium White Beauty, the reflexed petals and yellow anthers showing up so well against the rich foliage. One of the most desirable 'blues' is *Triteleia uniflorum* Wisley Blue, seen at its best in drifts amongst shrubs.

The early faithfuls, aubretia, alyssum, arabis and iberis (candytuft) are a mass of colour on the walls and in the paving. Although rampant growers, they are true country garden plants, bridging the gap between daffodils and the first summer flowers. The tight carpets of *Phlox subulata* are also studded with flower. No garden should be without this plant: the vigorous *P. s.* Marjory is excellent cascading over large stones and walls, its deep pink flowers so abundantly displayed; White Delight is pure white over compact apple green foliage; but the real charmer is G. F. Wilson, with cool lavender flowers and darker centres.

A mass of green shoots appear in the bog garden, *Iris pseudacorus*, the yellow water flag, already 30cm (1ft) high, along with varieties of *Iris sibirica*. Seedlings of *Mimulus luteus* spring up everywhere, and white stems of the water mint creep through shallow water. The fine golden yellow cups of *Caltha palustris* strike a cheery note against the lavender drumsticks of *Primula denticulata*. We are fortunate that the bog garden is on a large scale that can allow numerous plantings of the giant rhubarb *Rheum palmatum* and the prickly rhubarb *Gunnera manicata*, their sheer size and majestic leaf formations creating a never-to-be-forgotten effect in summer.

A new primula bed where the rockery merges into the bog garden has been a great success. The first groups of *Primula rosea* Grandiflora, *P. japonica* and selected forms of *P. denticulata* seem happy in the moist conditions, and to these we have added *P. florindae*, the giant Himalayan cowslip, and *P. Inshriach* hybrids which contain some grand orange and deep red shades. The potential is of course unlimited and we are already raising further varieties from seed.

In the pool garden a long sheltered border against a warm rose-covered wall is devoted entirely to paeonies, both single and double varieties, as well as numerous clumps of *Paeonia mlokosewitschii*, a Caucasian species of great merit. Its young ruby-red spears are already well advanced and support will soon be needed. For this we have a supply of the old-fashioned paeony rings, consisting of two well-spaced circular rings welded to three extended legs, a choice of

The lower waterfall in the rock garden, with *Primula denticulata* in the foreground three sizes ideally containing the loose habit of this plant. The framework is completely hidden by adequate summer leaves.

I am never in too much of a rush to trim back plants that rely on new growth to provide flowers, and this year especially I delayed this task until now. These plants include fuchsias and penstemons, *Perovskia atriplicifolia* Blue Spire and *Caryopteris* × *clandonensis*, hypericum Hidcote variety and *H.* × Rowallane. One or two less hardy plants that suffer from frost also need pruning back to new growth. It is an ideal time for the removal of dead or injured wood from trees and shrubs, and while this routine task is being carried out we become aware of various plants that, although not eye-catching, are yet individually interesting. *Salix melanostachys* against a north wall sports catkins that are almost black before turning yellow; *Acer palmatum* Dissectum starts to unfurl its finely cut green leaves; and under a sheltered wall *Daphne odora* Aureomarginata bears clusters of its fragrant pink flowers. Where should we be without these walls?

In a gritty pocket of the rock garden that charming little thrift *Armeria caespitosa* attracts many insects to its pale pink flowers, and the primrose-yellow heads of *Saxifraga* × *apiculata* are also borne freely. *Arabis ferdinandi-coburgi* produces a few white flowers, but as a

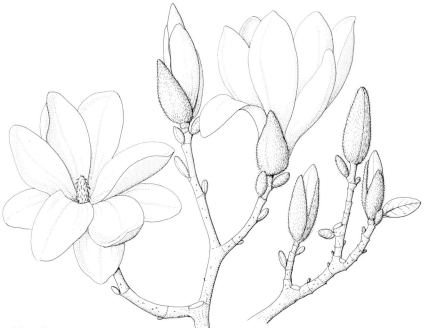

Magnolia × *soulangeana*

foliage plant for the scree or rock garden it is superb, the cream and gold leaves creating a striking effect. *Iris stylosa* enjoys a dry spot under an old buddleia as its season of flowering wanes, while across the lawn the swollen buds of *Magnolia* × *soulangeana* remind us, with a glimpse of white petal, that spring is not too far away.

Nature can be cruel, for on the 25th we were hit by sudden snowstorms in the late afternoon, bringing arctic conditions and huge drifts. Fierce winds drove freezing snow through the valley, leaving a trail of destruction and cutting the electricity supply to the village. Weeping willows were decapitated, a specimen copper beech, *Fagus sylvatica* Riversii, split in two, cherries burned black, and a huge old wild cherry, *Prunus avium*, was completely uprooted by sheer weight of snow and ice. It gave us two weeks' extra work that we could well do without, just clearing away the aftermath of a freak storm.

Under glass, temperatures fluctuate as sunny days quickly rise to 18°C (65°F), but drop to the minimum of 4.5°C (40°F) at night with continued frost. To reduce the effect of the two extremes the houses are ventilated whenever possible, deferring opening until 10am and always closing down by 4pm to retain daylight warmth.

Pans of seeds on the warming bench have germinated rapidly and now require a few days' hardening away from heat before being pricked out or individually potted. The first sowings of tomatoes are almost 5cm (2in) high, sturdy dark green plants with that slight tinge of purple in the stem I like to see. Potted in 9cm (3½in) pots, they will make rapid growth from now on, especially if the atmosphere is kept turgid for a day or two, and should be ready for planting in the tomato house by the end of the month.

The outdoor tomato is supreme for flavour, so in addition to the indoor crop, which meets all needs and a surplus for sale, I grow a dozen plants of a small-fruited variety – I find the thin-skinned Small Fry most suitable – for outside cultivation. They are indispensable for summer salads, yielding ropes of marble-sized fruit from August onwards. Seeds are sown now to produce strong plants for June planting. When large enough they are moved into 9cm (3½in) pots, and have a further move into 12.5cm (5in) pots as roots develop. This is followed by a careful hardening-off period in cold frames with a further spell against a sheltered wall before they are planted out in the warmest position possible when conditions are favourable. By this method an extra month of growing season is gained, enabling a large proportion of the fruit to ripen before the approach of autumn.

Petunia Carnival and the cascading Jamboree mixture, along with lobelia Cambridge Blue and Blue Cascade, are pricked out forty to the box. Dianthus Magic Charms are already making sturdy little plants and, together with the above, are transferred to the frames at the end of the month. Inevitably a few gaps appear in the large borders and to compensate I sow now pans of dwarf aster, annual coreopsis, cosmea and zinnia; all make useful fillers for planting out in May and considerably extend late season colour.

Almost any kind of greenhouse plant can be propagated this month, as and when material is available. First and foremost is *Campanula isophylla*, so adaptable to the role of basket-filler or for decoration indoors, and worth a gamble as a plant for outside flower tubs. Stock plants are kept through the winter with minimal watering, and are soon induced into growth by a thorough soaking of the soil ball and fresh soil worked into the surface. Division is also possible, but plants raised from cuttings are more vigorous and free flowering. As well as the blue form there is a charming white form, *C. i.* Alba, a strong grower with smaller dark leaves, and *C. i.* Mayii with variegated foliage and pale lavender cups.

Foliage plants are always needed as a back-up to flowering plants and so often they are associated with the warm house. The *Tradescantia* family provide many variations, the best plants coming from freshly propagated stock as they are seldom worth keeping after a year. *Tradescantia* Rochfords Quicksilver, with silver and green leaves, is so vigorous that mature plants can be had in less than three months, and it has the added merit of not reverting to green. The purple-leaved *T. purpurea* is a great contrast, as is *T. setcreasia purpusii*, with deeper colouring and upright habit, but for colour combinations the closely-related green-, white- and red-striped *Zebrina pendula tricolour* is unbeatable. All these varieties increase readily from cuttings inserted in fine sand.

In shady situations there is no better plant for foliage effect than *Plectranthus australis*, whose waxy green leaves will happily tumble over from pots or baskets. *P. coleoides* Marginata is smaller-leaved with a green and yellow variegation, excellent for indoor and outdoor decoration. Both are increased by soft cuttings in spring.

Where space permits, the Madeira Vine, *Boussingaltia basilloides*, will make a handsome plant with trailing stems of 2m (6ft) or more and white flowers. Because of its doubtful hardiness it is wise to keep a stock plant of *Helichrysum petiolatum* under glass. Cuttings struck now will produce strong plants for early June planting in some of our stone urns, where the gently curved branches covered with felted grey leaves are an invaluable asset. Spare plants are not wasted, for in paving and along path edges they are great softeners of hard lines.

Begonias and gloxinias trayed up last month have made new growth and can now be placed directly into 12.5cm (5in) pots. They prefer a well-drained acid compost, and in the case of begonias it is advisable to set the corms fairly low in the pot to allow for a topping up process as growth proceeds. In all their forms, single, double and trailing, the flowers can be much admired under glass, but alas they are not a subject that lend themselves to indoor use.

Much more accommodating are some of the fibrous rooted species, *Begonia sutherlandii*, *B. fuchsioides* and the richly foliaged *B. rex. Begonia sutherlandii* I find irresistible, and a large batch is grown in 9cm (3½ in) pots for bedroom and hall decoration at the manor. The red-stemmed, light green leaves and the tiny single orange flowers last well into the autumn as long as they are protected from direct sunlight. Small bulbils are formed in the leaf axils in autumn, and these are collected and stored in dry sand for the winter. Placed in a sandy peat and just covered, they quickly form fresh little rosettes, especially over bottom heat.

Achimenes rhizomes are sending up new shoots and must soon be potted on. Six in a 12.5cm (5in) pot make a wonderful splash of colour, or they can be potted singly for individual effect. They need a fibrous compost with ample peat or leafmould and not too firm a potting, and throughout their life they must be shaded from strong sunshine. These conditions also apply to smithianthas, and both need careful watering in the early stages followed by an abundance of water in summer.

I would be the first to admit that the chrysanthemum reigns supreme for autumn and winter display, yet I have never worked up any great enthusiasum for growing them. Through the necessity to supply tall subjects for decoration, we grow a number in large pots, mainly Spidery forms and the single Mason's Bronze. Much more pleasing to the eye in my way of thinking are the cascade-type Charm chrysanthemums and the recently introduced FI Autumn Queen mixture. Both are easily raised from seed this month, potted singly when large enough and transferred to the cold frame. These plants branch naturally and only one stopping is necessary to help them form a well rounded bush. In June they are planted outside, when, without the construction of pots, they will form mounds a metre wide for lifting in early autumn.

A mullein admirably suited to the cool house is *Celsia arcturus*, bearing a succession of yellow flowers enhanced by purple anthers on its branching stems. Given cool, airy conditions it will flower for three months or more, and as a house plant it is very acceptable.

Calceolarias are bursting into bloom, their delightfully marked pouched flowers coming in so many colours from modern strains of seed. These make fine specimen plants in 15cm (6in) pots, the compact and self supporting multiflora type being most suitable. Indoor conditions do not suit them, and though they are much admired they are unfortunately short lived.

A number of plants that need large pots for their final stages include *Campanula pyramidalis, Humea elegans* and *Trachelium coeruleum.* Some wallflowers and myosotis lifted earlier in the month and potted are showing flower and will provide extra subjects for the house. Other plants in flower include amaryllis and *Jasminum primulinum,* pelargoniums and the last of the azaleas, *Billbergia nutans* and primroses. Seeds to sow now are *Torenia fournieri, Celosia argentea* Plumosa, *Didiscus caeruleus* and balsam.

The bromeliads are a diverse and complex group of plants normally requiring higher temperatures than ours, but one member that will tolerate much cooler conditions is *Billbergia nutans.* In a pot-bound state the large sharp edged leaves give rise to bright pink bracts from which emerge seven or more narrow tubular flowers that

Billbergia nutans

are striped green and mauve. The tube opens to three purple-edged leaves and long yellow anthers, a remarkable colour combination. They demand shade at all times, especially during the flowering season of April and May, and they are easily increased by the numerous offsets that will root readily in sandy peat over gentle bottom heat.

Having accepted that our 'spring' will be late this year, it is easy to concentrate one's thoughts and efforts on the other parts of the garden and shelve the enormous amount of work that will pesent itself in the kitchen garden. The routine work I leave to Norman, who is totally involved in it, but when conditions are suitable a combined effort from all of us is often necessary. By no means could one man cope with the volume of work that descends upon us in April. A break from the incessant rain at last gives the earth a chance to dry, and warmth from the sun coupled with drying winds visibly changes the colour and texture of the soil. Just when we start to cultivate to produce a tilth cannot be easily explained – it is a matter of experience and touch.

At certain times of the year the rotovator is a much overrated machine, but for working the ground to a tilth during the next few weeks it is unquestionably invaluable. It is now that the chore of winter digging and manuring can be fully appreciated as the earth breaks down to a fine texture.

Preparation of a good seed bed is all important. If space allows, as it does here, it is sound husbandry to move to a fresh area each year, applying a little superphosphate a few weeks in advance. The majority of sowings are made in the open without any form of protection. There comes a morning when, by instinct, we know the ground is in prime condition. Not only do we have to sow all varieties of vegetables for summer and autumn use; the very fact that the season is late necessitates the planning of half-hardy and winter varieties in the very near future. Correct labelling eliminates any doubt about what has been sown where more than one person is involved, and evenly and thinly sown seed will produce strong sturdy plants.

Watch our for leaf-eating insects and slugs – prevention is better than cure. Wood pigeons can be a menace here as well as ring doves, as so often they take a liking to young seedlings. We have a number of frames covered with fine netting that can be moved over at a moment's notice. For larger areas the scarecrow is still one of the best deterrents – modern inventions have yet to convince me. Rabbits, too, we have plenty of, but fortunately the surrounding

Espaliered pear Conference in blossom in the kitchen garden

walls prevent them from getting in. We just pray that nobody will leave any of the doors open one night.

The first sowing of peas is always a pleasant task: perhaps it is the thought of summer pickings that spur us on. Good deep preparation is absolutely vital. Trenches a spade's width and 5cm (2in) deep are taken out and a general fertiliser worked into the soil before a triple row is sown. For these early sowings I use Progress No 9, a prolific cropper, and Kelvedon Wonder for its fine flavour.

Salad crops are constantly in demand during the summer, and the keynote to supply is carefully planned sowings in succession. The length of a row across our garden is 24m (80ft), and for spring onions, radish and lettuce a third of a row is sown at fortnightly intervals. For early radishes, with or without cloches, I recommend Rota, a variety producing top quality round red roots, and for later sowing Sparkler and the ever popular French Breakfast.

The mild flavour and rapid growth of White Lisbon make this variety the traditionally sown spring onion. Lettuce is a matter of personal choice. Many varieties which are offered with resistance to mildew and tipburn afford some help to the private gardener. To follow Tom Thumb I find the cos Little Gem and butterhead Avoncrisp are the most suitable, as they both withstand the cooler conditions which so often occur in May.

At long last we are able to drill two rows of parsnips Tender and True, along with half a row of Early Nantes carrots. This variety can be pulled young, when the cylindrical roots are of superb flavour. From the cold frames, and after a period of hardening, cabbage June

Star and cauliflower Dok Elgon are planted out for July maturing.

As the ground dries out and becomes workable with several passes of rotovation, it is time to think about planting early potatoes. Normally the second or third week this month is an ideal time, especially if the tubers have been trayed out and allowed to form 12mm (½ in) long sprouts, but there is no sense and certainly no gain in planting in cold wet soil. Pentland Javelin and Sutton's Foremost are the first to go in, they are well tried in this garden and can be relied upon to crop well. I still look forward to lifting the first roots and presenting the first basket of delicious medium-sized white potatoes to the kitchen.

It is onion-planting time, and in a bed of six hundred half are grown from sets and the other half from autumn- and spring-sown seed. The variety Sturon produces excellent onions from sets and normally stores well until Christmas, but for long-term storage of quality bulbs our autumn-sown Bedfordshire Champion and spring-sown Balstora prove most suitable. For a mild-flavoured onion I would strongly recommend the red-skinned Southport Red Globe. Whilst on the subject of onions, a sowing of the Japanese FI Express Yellow made last August has produced an excellent row of small hardy bulbs which will now benefit by a top dressing of nitrogenous fertiliser to swell them up for early July lifting. I find these sharp-flavoured onions well worth growing and invaluable for bridging the gap until the maincrop is harvested.

I have not yet fully convinced the kitchen that celeriac is as delicious a vegetable as I think it is. Its many uses include soup flavouring and as a stew ingredient, and it is much liked diced with turnip. Needless to say, I grow increasing quantities every year, and along with celery raised under glass last month, the plants are pricked out into trays and placed in the cold frame.

Mid-April is none too early to raise the first batch of sweet corn in the gentle warmth of the greenhouse. Seeds are sown singly in 9cm (3½ in) pots, and when growth is about 2.5cm (1in) high they are transferred to the frame. One hundred and fifty plants supply sufficient cobs for fresh table use and for freezing, the crop being divided into the early and mid-season varieties Early King and Seneca Star. This early start not only guarantees that plants are well forward when planted out in June, but also that they receive the maximum sunshine when most needed.

A further row of broad beans will ensure succession in picking – theoretically, that is, for, as is often the case, the higher soil temperatures encountered this month will produce quicker growth resulting in the narrowest of gaps between early and late sowings.

Cloches are placed over a ten-metre strip to warm the soil in preparation for an early sowing of dwarf beans in May. Early pickings of this delicate-flavoured bean are much appreciated, though their popularity wanes with the approach of the first runner beans. A 24m (80ft) double row, by any standard, is a lot of runner beans, and to spread the picking season over as long a time as possible we raise the first sixty plants in the frames for planting next month.

The seed bed has been raked out to a workable tilth and the following seeds are sown immediately: Brussels sprouts Peer Gynt, to produce buttons from November onwards; cabbage Stonehead and Minicole, both these varieties standing well at maturity and remaining in good condition for several weeks; red cabbage for pickling during the winter and a pinch of cauliflower Islandia for succession. Early leek The Lyon and maincrop Winter Reuzen are both sown now, and also cos lettuce Lobjoits Green and cabbage type lettuce Webbs Wonderful.

MAY

In sheltered places there seems to be some response to the occasional warm day, but understandably there is a general reluctance of many subjects to burst into growth whilst cold rains and rimy frost persist. Even under these conditions the garden takes on a vastly different appearance in the month of May: winter blackness of trees disappears as buds unfurl, and the harsh lines of walls and paving soften as new growth quickly spreads.

The recuperative powers of most trees is amazing after last month's havoc. Cherries and crabs continue to delight us with their blossom. The multi-petalled flowers and early bronze foliage of *Prunus* Kanzan temporarily dominate the garden, while *P.* Shimidsu Sakura, at the top of the church walk, covers its spreading horizontal branches with long-stalked clusters of pure white flowers, the pale bronze leaves accentuating the beauty of this fine cherry.

Malus floribunda, deservedly planted in many Cotswold gardens, can always be relied on to cover its rather untidy arching branches with clouds of apple-blossom flowers, but for me the darker-leaved varieties such as Lemoinei, Eleyi and – probably the most spectacular – Profusion, with their crimson flowers, make beautiful contrasts of colour in the woodland. By the kitchen entrance we have an old tree of *M.* John Downie, leaning away from the north winds and more attractive in fruit than in flower. Its orange and red 'apples', which it abundantly produces in September, make fine crab-apple jelly.

That eminent gardener, the late Marjory Fish, once wrote: 'Gardeners with walls can get much of their work done for them,' and with this I would agree with certain reservations, we have so much wall space here at Cornwell, that it would be one man's job alone to look after the walls were every bit clothed with climbing plants. As the month progresses the south- and east-facing walls of the manor become alive with colour. The yellow Banks's rose, *Rosa banksiae* Lutea, almost covers the south wall with its clusters of double lemon-yellow flowers so freely borne. Through necessity, I limit its height to 6m (20ft) by a light pruning in September. At the extremity of the wall the first pink blooms of climbing rose Madame Grégoire Staechelin are opening, while its neighbour Madame Alfred Carrière carries buds of the palest pink opening to white. These are two charming climbers, the volume of early flowers compensating for their reluctance to bear a second crop of flowers.

Round the corner to the east, two *Ceanothus* × *veitchianus* climb to the roof either side of the French windows. This must be one of the hardiest members of a suspect family; even after the cold winter of 1978, when they were blackened and pronounced a loss, they recovered to clothe the wall once again with rich powder-blue flowers the following summer. They also act as hosts to other climbers. After rambling up behind the support wires to a height of 3m (10ft), *Clematis macropetala* cascades down with nodding blue cups, and the attractive foliage and fragrant chocolate-purple flowers of *Akebia quinata* and the blood-red cydonia *Chaenomeles speciosa* Simonii are also prominent, along with other roses.

In the courtyard the walls are tall enough to accommodate the vigorous *Clematis montana* and its pink counterpart *C. m.* Pink Perfection, both producing huge quatities of flower over their serrated foliage.

An arched gateway leading to the kitchen garden is encircled by honeysuckle, but from its dense growth appear long twining stems of *Actinidia kolomikta*, whose tricoloured foliage of white, pink and purple tints fascinates all who see it.

April's storms laid low almost all the bulbous subjects, the survivors in a protected corner of the Spring garden being *Narcissus* Actaea and Laurens Koster. The lawns, too, after a good start have lost some of their freshness, quickly noticeable on our shallow land, so now is an excellent time to top-dress them with a fertiliser to restore colour and promote the growth of fine grasses.

Hybrid tea and floribunda roses have had a rough passage since pruning. Some early foliage has been nipped by the frost, and there has been die-back on leading shoots, necessitating additional pruning back to firm growth. The first of the top dressings with a good organic fertiliser can be applied now. In fact, as frosts are mild and the ground is warming, it is an ideal time to apply fertiliser to many different plants to set them up for the growing season.

Flower tubs on the terrace are a splash of colour against the grey balustrading, with wallflower Cranford Beauty, a bright yellow, interplanted with the red hybrid Darwin tulip Holland's Glory. Stone urns are topped with the myosotis (forget-me-not) Blue Ball.

The great advantage of a large garden is that an area can be

(*Left*) 'Boy and Serpents', a statue and fountain whose lines merge well with the background of stepped terraces up to the old park gates. (*Right*) Silver foliage and white flowers of *Pyrus salicifolius* Pendula grace the banks of the canal

devoted to one genus or perhaps one particular plant, but my great love for all plants, be it an aconite or a chestnut tree, inevitably leads to mixed plantings. In many cases foliage outshines flower, so before the rush of June colour it is the fresh leaves and stems of deciduous shrubs that I rely on for good effect. I think one of the finest examples is *Sambucus racemosa* Plumosa Aurea, the finely cut leaves of gold so bright even on a dull day. The best coloured foliage comes from new growth, which means hard but sensible pruning in March; a little shade is also appreciated. Nearby we have an old sprawling *Phlomis fruticosa*, the Jerusalem sage, whose soft grey will live with most colours including the brilliant red new leaves of *Berberis thunbergii* Somerset. A few years ago I purchased a young *B. t.* aurea, only to be greatly disappointed by its subsequent growth and colour, and it was not until I recently spoke to an expert on this family that I understood its hate for wind and full sun. Having had both, it was moved into a walled garden in the shade of a *Viburnum tinus*, and now I can appreciate to the full its beautiful pale-golden foliage.

73

The dogwoods have year-round appeal, especially the red-stemmed varieties so noticeable in winter. Among the most effective this month are *Cornus alba* Elegantissima with striped grey-green and white foliage, and *C. a.* Spaethii with its lovely green and golds. I have a sneaking regard for *C. stolonifera* Flaviramea; its soft green leaves are not so eye-catching as some, but planted here against *Prunus laurocerasus*, its yellow-ochre stems are outstanding in winter.

For a sheer brazen splash, *Spiraea × bumalda* Goldflame remains unique. Of fairly recent introduction, this plant treats us to a startling display of old-gold spring leaves before mellowing in summer; crimson flowers also add interest to this foliage plant.

Fuchsias are invaluable for a late summer show, continuing to flower until blackened by October frost. Many are reliably hardy when once established, and among them is a variety that precedes its arching stems with early foliage that defies a true colour description. I refer to *Fuchsia magellanica gracilis* Versicolor, with its shades of grey and cream, pink and carmine, a much underrated plant that will give pleasure for six months of the year.

Always on the lookout for interesting hardy plants, I remember John had praised the qualities of *Prunus × cistena* after seeing them at Edinburgh Botanic Gardens. We planted one, and now I must agree that it is a first-class addition, its red stems and rich crimson leaves forming a great contrast against the white flowers. Other newly planted items this year are a dwarf mountain ash, *Sorbus reducta*, *Spiraea japonica* Snowmound, *Ceanothus impressus* and *Spiraea japonica* Alpina, a compact dwarf shrub with tiny leaves and pink flowers.

It is on my numerous visits to that great plantsman Percy Picton in the Malvern Hills that I find one or two unusual plants. His son Paul assured me that *Viburnum tomentosum* Semperflorens Nanum would flower all summer, so we shall see. On seeing a specimen *Ceanothus arboreus* with huge panicles of electric-blue flowers, I knew I must possess one, knowing full well that it is on the borderline of hardiness and prone to frost and wind damage – but who could resist it?

I find a day at the Chelsea Flower Show infinitely more tiring than a hard day's work in the garden, yet it presents such a vast array of plants, old and new, grown to perfection, that the professional gardener can ill afford to miss it. Unfortunately, it is so well patronised these days that the sheer enjoyment of standing and observing the skill and artistry of it all is overidden by the mass of pushing people, presenting, I'm sure, increasing difficulties to the Royal Horticultural Society.

The early flush of spring bulbs in the rock garden has slowly died away, to be followed now by a surge of spring-flowering alpines planted amongst dwarf conifers and shrubs. Dry sloping banks, shaded shelves among grey stone and moist pockets influenced by cascading water provide a home for a great diversity of plants. Prominent are the elegant dwarf aquilegias, *A. flabellata* Nana, just 10cm (4in) high with blue and white flowers, and the white form *A. f.* Nana Alba, both from Japan, as well as the short spurred bright blue *A. alpina*. A drift of *Veronica gentianoides* with its pale blue spikes is a pleasing sight, although quick to fade, and likewise the variegated form of slightly deeper colour. Both are holders of the AGM (Award of Garden Merit) and worthy of a place in the large rock garden or border front. A contrast to the pink thrifts is the white form *Armeria maritima alba*, flowering well on a spartan diet. Similar conditions suit *Onosma alboroseum*, a 'grey' with sharp hairy leaves and sprays of white flowers that turn pink with age. In full sun the rich yellow cups of *Ranunculus gramineus* will continue to bloom for many weeks, whilst in semi-shade the gentian blue pulmonaria Rob Roy seems quite happy under *Cryptomeria japonica elegans*. A metre wide mat of the phlox Scarlet Flame tumbles over a rock face, and with other varieties such as Temiscaming and Alexander's Surprise it provides the bulk of colour this month.

Other gems in flower include *Aethionema* × Warley Rose, *Leucojum aestivum*, the summer snowflake, *Linum capitatum*, *Oxalis adenophylla*, *Geranium sanguineum lancastriense* and *Phlox doughlasii* Lilac Queen. Attractive all the year round, the silver saxifrages – both the white Dr Ramsey and the creamy Esther – are reliable free-flowerers, as also is *Saxifraga aizoon rosea*.

Mossy saxifrage James Bremner, a magnificent wall plant. The white flowers need semi-shade to be seen at their best

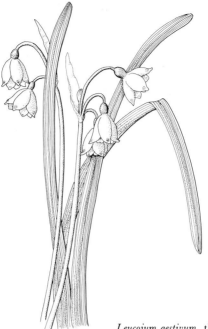

Leucojum aestivum, the Summer Snowflake

Without a doubt this is the busiest month of the year under glass, ideally warranting one man's undivided attention to keep abreast of the work. This, of course, is not possible as outside pressures are equally high. Priority must go to the completion of planting in the tomato house; the early batch of Alicante in the open bed show obvious signs of healthy activity both above and below ground and carry two trusses of flower. It is now that the careful preparation of the bed undertaken six weeks ago really begins to pay off with roots enjoying the humus content and the base fertiliser supplying the necessary nutrients for two or three weeks. March sowings of MM and Tangella have quickly filled the 9cm (3½in) pots with roots and are now ready for their final move into 25cm (10in) pots. The basis for pot culture compost must be well rotted fibrous turf and on no account must it 'pan', preventing fine root development. To see the house completely planted up with plants in various stages of growth is a fine sight, for with it comes the expectancy of ripe fruit in the months to come and the realisation that the all-important cultural routine of watering, feeding and tying has only just begun.

Temperature and ventilation control is vital, so I allow the heating system to just tick over, giving that little extra warmth and air movement that prevent any check in growth, and at the same time ensuring active root growth.

76

Interest grows in the plant house as several species come in to flower to form our spring display. Outstanding in colour and form, the clivia or Kaffir lily must rate very highly as one of the most beautiful plants for a cool house. At these temperatures they need very little water from October to March, just enough to prevent the soil from becoming dust dry, and an occasional leaf-sponging with lukewarm water. This rest under dry conditions is the keynote to flower production. Being of South African origin, they need all the sunshine possible, and visibly respond to warm spring days. When the tight congested flower buds can be seen nosing their way through the leathery leaves it is time to be generous with both watering and feeding. This is one plant that needs to be pot bound, and a strong clay pot is necessary to contain the mass of fleshy roots. Stems rise to 60cm (2ft) or more, topped by an umbel of pale orange white-throated flowers. It is not a true house plant, but given a sunny window it will remain a picture of colour for at least three weeks.

The responsibility for supplying the mainstay of flowering plants for decoration this month rests with the Regal pelargonium. What splendid floriferous and diversely coloured plants they are. I'm quite sure that they would prefer a degree or two more warmth in the

Clivia or Kaffir lily

winter than our minimum 4.5°C (40°F), yet kept on the dry side they struggle bravely through to warmer days. During March they grow rapidly and need a 12.5cm (5in) pot or larger to produce specimen plants. Although reasonably happy with soilless compost, they have a tendency to make oversoft growth, and it is for this reason that I use John Innes No 2 or a similar loam-based mixture to encourage firm growth and, inevitably, longer-lasting flowers. Varieties are too numerous to list, but to single out favourites I would have to mention Grandma Fischer, bright orange with a brown blotch, and the wine-red Burgundy.

Another plant I rely heavily on for the next few months is *Trachelium coeruleum*. Its free-flowering qualities and easy culture put it in the forefront of pot plants, and as it is almost hardy the season of flowering can be regulated by frequent sowings. By far the best results are made from a July sowing. By October they will be strong plants in 12.5cm (5in) pots, then during March or April they need a final move to a 20cm (8in) pot and regular feeding when the fine roots develop. Frequent pinching out of the leading shoots will ensure a bushy habit, and when the flowering stems start to elongate some support is necessary. This method will result in fine specimens up to 1.5m (5ft) high, graced by dense large heads of tiny blue flowers giving a hazy gypsophila-like effect. Lasting well in the house, especially in big airy rooms, they are always admired, and as long as feeding and copious watering continues they will flower for many weeks. Alternatively, sowings made from March onwards will produce smaller but equally valuable plants for late summer and autumn flowering.

Standard fuchsias are growing strongly and now need a move to their final pots. The compost, whatever the components, must be sharply drained and slightly acidic. My own preference is for seven parts loam, four parts peat, one part sand and one part fine grit, with the addition of a base fertiliser. If the loam is known to be alkaline, incorporate an ounce of flowers of sulphur to the bushel. The attractiveness of fuchsias to whitefly has led to verbal condemnation of them on many occasions both from myself and my staff, yet all is forgiven when they burst into flower, showing delicate colouring in countless permutations. Unfortunately, they do not take kindly to indoor conditions; their enemy is a dry atmosphere that quickly crisps the foliage. A change of plants every week is necessary, but even so, some varieties are more tolerant than others. In standard form the salmon and carmine Coachman along with the popular Snowcap are excellent, while for trailing effect Swingtime and the smaller-flowered La Campenella look charming casading

Snowcap, an excellent fuchsia for training as a standard, is particularly noted for its prolific flowering

down from tall containers. Thalia, with its long tubes of orangy scarlet borne in clusters, makes an eye-catching bush.

Almost without exception, greenhouse plants require protection from the direct rays of the sun and some form of shading by the end of the month. Both the plant house and the propagating house had slatted wooden roller blinds in days gone by, but nothing lasts for ever and now all that remains are one or two selected pieces which are very useful for frame shading. A shading compound called

Coolglass is very efficient and permanent, and can be removed at the end of the season with a dry cloth.

To try and cater for the needs of all the plants we grow, half of each of these two houses is shaded completely, while the other half is roof-shaded only, thus, we hope, creating suitable conditions for the 'scorchers', such as begonia, gloxinia and streptocarpus, as well as annual subjects such as trachelium, schizanthus and campanula.

Coleus seedlings pricked out into boxes earlier this month are now showing their leaf and colour forms, and the best are singled out and potted into 9cm (3½ in) pots. I can never have too many, and only lack of space prevents me from growing them in quantity. A few dark-coloured forms with a paler edging are trained as small standards, and what a beautiful effect they create in a mixed arrangement.

As space becomes available there are more seeds to sow to provide pot plants in the early autumn and following spring. Just a pinch of seed of each variety is all that is necessary for annuals such as schizanthus, celosia, browallia and torenia. Some useful foliage plants can also be raised from seed, such as *Cyperus alternifolius, Dracaena indivisa, Schefflera digitata* and, the most useful of all, *Grevillea robusta.* Some patience is called for in the germination of this 'silk oak'; I have known it appear in less than a week and on other occasions take three months, but subsequently its silvery bronze-green, finely cut leaves make it a first rate subject for a cool house.

Also readily raised from seed are the ornamental varieties of asparagus fern, *Asparagus plumosus nanus* and *A. sprengeri.* Both are indispensable for decoration and are elegant plants all the year round. The seeds have a hard shell, and soaking them for twenty four hours in warm water will greatly assist germination, as long as a bottom heat of 18°C (65°F) can be maintained.

For fragrance and colour few plants can compete with the freesia, and by far the best way to provide stems for cutting in the gloomy days of winter is to raise them from seed. The seeds are, again, hard coated so, to assist germination, I roll them gently between two pieces of fine sandpaper until some of the shell begins to crack away, and then stand them in tepid water for two days. Germination is usually erratic, but if the seeds are placed in moist peat at about 15.5°C (60°F) they become active, and as they sprout they can be carefully transferred to deep boxes or pots.

Pans of rooted cuttings of *Campanula isophylla, Helichrysum petiolatum,* fuchsias and *Begonia fuchsioides* await potting, and a never-ending number of plants need potting on – impatiens, *Exacum affine,* solanums and streptocarpus.

As day temperatures rise the true growing season begins, and a regular programme of spraying and fumigation becomes necessary to keep disease and pests at bay. But above all, the watering and feeding requirements of each individual plant should be clearly understood.

Morning frost is now quickly dispersed by warmer days, and we have conditions that bring joy to all gardeners. We should like to think that we can put behind us the bitter winds and driving rain so prevalent in April, but at the back of our minds we know only too well that it can all return overnight. Snow showers are not uncommon in the Cotswolds during May, yet to be over-cautious now – probably the busiest month of the year in the kitchen garden – can often lead to a serious gap in the calendar of cropping.

The soil is warm and friable, and a concerted effort by all sees the remainder of maincrop potatoes planted. It would seem ironic to all but a gardener that already we are thinking in terms of crops a year ahead from now. Purple sprouting and white sprouting broccoli must be sown now to produce strong plants that will stand up to all that next winter can test them with. In the same family is the delicous calabrese broccoli, which must also be sown during May for late summer use. Cloche or frame protection can mean an earlier crop, but as we have an abundance of fresh vegetables in mid-summer I prefer to plan maturity for September onwards. Great strides have been made in the breeding of varieties suitable to our climate; the early Green Comet is just one that gives good succulent green heads and Corvette is excellent to continue the season into autumn.

Summer salads seem incomplete without tender young beetroot. In warmer gardens April sowings are commonplace, but here I delay until now. Germination is rapid if the soil has been well worked and firmed, and a little extra time spent on evenly spaced sowing will eliminate the necessity of thinning. A third of a row is sown every two weeks, maintaining a supply of tender roots throughout the summer and autumn. My choice for both early and later crops is Boltardy, for not only is it resistant to bolting but also it is a variety of excellent colour and quality.

Too early a sowing of late Brussels sprouts can easily result in varieties maturing all at the same time, and for this reason I delay sowing until now the FI hybrids Ladora and Rampart. This is often also the case with winter cabbage, producing a glut around December. To minimise this annoying state of affairs, I sow small quantities of four varieties between now and early June. To follow

81

Minicole, which stands so well, I use Christmas Drumhead and the ever reliable January King. For the depths of winter I shall try Celtic once again and Bartolo, highly recommended to me for later heading.

As well as further sowings of cauliflower Dok Elgon for September–October use, I also include some sowings of Islandia. They could well mature together but the latter has strong erect foliage affording good protection in adverse weather. Looking further ahead, winter cauliflowers must be sown during the last week of May. I plan for April and May heading, using April Queen and May Blossom, both of which are 'English Winter' selections.

A further sowing of lettuce is due and conditions are suitable for one of my favourites, Continuity. What a beautiful crisp lettuce it is, unusual in appearance with red-tinged outer leaves, yet for flavour it is matched only by cos Little Gem.

Preparatory work is all important for many crops, none more so than celery. By no stretch of the imagination is this celery land, as I have stated earlier, but we continue to try. The trench we prepare now is only 30cm (1ft) deep with some well rotted compost worked into the brash. A few centimetres of soil is returned and a balanced fertiliser applied.

Runner beans sown in boxes last month are stood outside for a period of hardening off before planting. The variety is Achievement, and this year's row is sited on rested ground. It takes John and Stuart almost a day to erect the framework and tie in the canes, a job that cannot be rushed, as the strength of the whole structure is vital. A dressing of fish, blood and bone is worked along the row before the boxed plants are set out during the third week. This accounts for approximately a third of the total plants, the remainder being raised from direct-sown seed.

Soil under cloches has warmed up for the first sowing of dwarf French beans The Prince, which will be followed by a further sowing in three weeks' time. The aim is to produce a nice batch of young beans leading up to the first of the runners.

The demand for peas is normally greater than the supply, and at weekly intervals four rows of Greenshaft are sown. With pods borne in pairs and tightly filled with ten or more small peas, this is a pea that suits our land very well. High yielding and of top quality, it provides the bulk for both kitchen use and freezing.

Although not so popular as they used to be, marrows still play an important role in the late summer cropping programme. They are perhaps more readily used in the form of courgettes when the flesh is tender. Nowadays it is possible to grow one variety for both stages, cutting the fruits early as courgettes or allowing them to mature as marrows. Early Gem and Green Bush are amongst those that are suitable. Eight plants produce all we need, and these are raised from seeds sown singly in pots under glass.

Last month's sowing of sweet corn under glass germinated quickly and the seedlings are now placed in the cold frames. When they have made about 15cm (6in) of growth they will stand outside in a sheltered position prior to planting out in June.

Further sowings of radish and spring onion are made now, along with turnip Golden Ball and further rows of carrot Amsterdam Forcing and Chantenay Red Cored.

Aside from the seasonal rush of seed-sowing there remains, as always, the question of the supply and demand of fresh vegetables for the kitchen. May is one of the leanest months for variety, and this year's atrocious spring weather has not helped the situation. Nevertheless, we have excellent heads of spring cabbage Flower of Spring and First Early Market, and what superb flavour and texture they have. A September sowing of winter lettuce Imperial is now producing some good heads and will, I am sure, be very acceptable. Purple sprouting and white sprouting broccoli are at their peak; we never seem to tire of their delicious young shoots, but picking must be daily now to prevent them running to seed. Rhubarb is ready by the armful, and surplus sticks are put down for freezing or jam making. Most disappointing is the asparagus. Weather conditions, as so often, have been against it all the way, and only a third of the stems are of table quality. How old the bed is I am not sure; the crowns are huge and woody, and over the next three years I shall be replacing them, initially with two-year crowns to be followed by seed-raised plants over a longer period.

A walk round the wall-trained trees and open orchards confirms my opinion that the April storm and late frosts have taken their toll of blossom. Insects, too, were almost non-existent. Contrary to other years, when plums and gages became almost an embarrassment, the next few weeks' weather will be vital for them. On the perimeters of the open orchards, the old trees of apple Laxton's Superb and Bramley Seedling have taken the full force of adverse weather and have afforded some measure of protection to the other trees. The young orchard in the kitchen garden has escaped the worst and will almost certainly bear heavy crops.

The overall picture is much healthier now, warmer days encouraging young plants to grow away quickly. After a long cold spring and many days with wet coats and numb fingers, the sun's warmth draws a wave of fresh enthusiasm from all of us.

JUNE

This month the kitchen garden enters a completely new phase of growing conditions. Frosts, if any, are of no substance, there is real power in the sun, and roughly dug earth is drying and crumbling and begging to be cultivated. Even the heavy-textured damp areas are changing colour as warm winds penetrate the ridges, and now respond to rotovation or hand cultivation.

Illogical though it may seem after a cold wet spring, some thought is given to our irrigation equipment. At half a spade's depth the soil remains wet and heavy and, combined with the moisture-retaining compost, will hold this level of wetness until at least mid-July. On the other hand, the top 5cm (2in) of earth containing a high stone content can dry out in a matter of a few days. It is for this reason that the water pump is checked and tested in good time, and as it was drained for the winter, it is normally only necessary to prime it and clean the intake pipe. The unlimited supply of natural water enables us to pump to five standing taps along the central path.

For the successful germination of seeds during the warmer months some form of additional moisture is most important, as we can seldom rely on rainfall completely. Our water pressure is a little below par – not nearly enough to drive the modern rotary or oscillating sprinkler – yet the much cheaper Hozelock type is excellent for vegetable work. The coverage is slightly reduced but the overall application is very even and without dry spots, and with the sprinkler mounted on a home-made 'skid' we are able to move it along the rows with a minimum of work.

Without a doubt it is a gratifying sight on a June morning, before the sun has dried the dew-laden earth, to see the long rows of young seedling vegetables that stretch across our garden. The seed bed is full of young plants ready for transplanting to their permanent position – winter cabbage, early and late Brussels sprouts, autumn cauliflowers and leeks. All brassicas need firm planting conditions and if the ground is at all 'spongy' we tread in the rows and then losen the surface with a cultivator.

Lonicera periclymenum Belgica intertwined with *Actinidia kolomikta* and clematis; the gateway leads to the cherry walk

Countless old stories about planting traditionally start with 'my grandfather', and vary from 30cm (12in) high monsters that are first de-rooted to plants being allowed to shrivel in the sun for a week. In some conditions these methods may well be practical, but I fail to see any great advantage in ill-treating young plants. My firm belief is that if a seedling is given a good start in receptive ground it will always produce the desired end result. Briefly, the transplants are thoroughly watered the evening before and moved the following morning, with a minimum of delay, to well-prepared ground that has had a dressing of fertiliser a few days previously. Firm planting followed by a puddling is essential, and if no rain falls within forty-eight hours the sprinkler is used.

Leeks require a rather special techinque; the friability and moisture content of the soil is of utmost importance, and planting should not commence until conditions are near perfect. We are limited to the depth of hole that a dibber can make by the shallowness of the land – 23cm (9in) is about average, but this will still produce excellent table-quality stems. They mature in the depths of winter, when they are always acceptable for their very individual flavour. Apart from watering in dry weather and keeping the surrounds clean, their needs are very modest.

The remainder of the runner beans are sown by the middle of the month, which should give us a long season of picking, but weather conditions are always the deciding factor. Plants from boxes have settled in well and are beginning to climb, having for once escaped the late frost. Insects are few in number; they too must have suffered from the cold spring and will be missed, just now, for pollinating the lower flowers of the beans.

Now fully hardened off, the pots of sweet corn are more than ready for planting out. They are grown in a block of 12 × 10, which not only assists fertilisation but later helps towards the stability of the plants. From the word go, they like as much sun as possible and a deep rich soil; but again it is false policy to advance the planting out unless warm conditions prevail.

I remember twenty years ago, when sweet corn was looked upon as a gamble which paid off only once in five years, but with the introduction of hybrid strains the maturing time has been brought into line with the English summer. If plants are raised under glass in late April there is no reason at all why delicious cobs cannot be picked from late August onwards.

Barn cloches are now removed from the early sowing of The Prince dwarf beans. In fact, all cloches except those over early strawberries are brought in. From the middle of the month onwards they serve no real purpose, having already given us early vegetables and advanced others by as much as a month. Young beans form rapidly and will now benefit by a free circulation of air and plenty of moisture; by the end of the month we should be picking tender pods. A time-consuming crop, they are readily accepted by the kitchen, as they fill an important gap until the runner beans come in. Then nobody wants them! During this month I sow a small row of Chevrier Vert, a most useful bean for picking in the green and intermediate stages of haricots as well as for drying for winter use.

Weekly sowings of pea Greenshaft are made during the month along with successional salad crops. There is now a ready supply of fresh vegetables, including the first of the true summer cauliflowers. From February sowings under glass Dok Elgon has produced firm white curds that need some protection from the sun by folding over a few of the large inner leaves. The winter-sown broad beans Seville Claudia are now ready and, picked at fingernail size, they are tender and possess a fine flavour. Strangely enough, they are not over popular in the fresh state; the surplus beans are frozen and it is during the winter that they are asked for.

The return of fresh salad crops is always eagerly awaited – young tender radish Rota, crisp and sweet lettuce Tom Thumb, and young pullings of spring onion White Lisbon. Further sowings of beetroot will be ready for late summer, and this also applies to turnip Snowball and carrot Early Nantes. Although never required in any quantity, both perpetual spinach and swede are extremely useful for early winter use and sowings of half a row are made now.

Celery plants are ready now for transplanting to the trench prepared a few weeks ago. We are ever hopeful for improved results but soil conditions and the pH content are against us from the start. Perhaps the breeders will one day produce a variety suitable for the Cotswolds.

Celeriac, on the other hand, will form excellent fat roots from plants put out now. As long as the land is in good heart and kept moist during dry spells they present no difficulties, and are a delicious vegetable by any standard.

Courgettes are generally more popular now than marrows, deservedly so I think, as flavour and texture is better and they lend themselves to more adventurous cooking. As soon as the nights become humid this month I plant out eight pot-grown plants of All Green Bush, a variety that can be cut as courgettes or allowed to mature into large marrows. This number of plants is more than adequate for our needs, many of the large specimens finishing up as decoration for the Harvest Festival.

The strawberry, of course, reigns supreme this month and into July. There is something about the first strawberry that can never be equalled for status in the kitchen garden, unless it is the first Cox's Orange Pippin. The second week sees a row under cloches producing luscious ripe fruit. Royal Sovereign is the variety, and personally I think it stands head and shoulders above all others for quality, size and flavour. Unprotected rows soon follow into fruit and for the first three weeks or so require daily picking every morning. We are always besieged by blackbirds at this time, making it imperative to protect our fruit with the netted frames that stand over 60cm (2ft) high and make picking relatively easy.

By the end of the month the first of the Careless gooseberries are ripening and provide a very welcome addition for the kitchen. This must be one of the finest varieties for both cooking and dessert, its vigorous habit greatly benefiting by fairly severe pruning in summer and winter.

In one of the busiest months of the year Norman needs some help every day to keep on top of the work. He is fully occupied sticking peas, earthing up the potatoes and perhaps most important of all, hoeing through all crops to control annual weeds, a task he really enjoys. To be amongst growing crops is, for him, happiness; to see baskets of freshly picked vegetables and punnets of soft fruit is just reward for his untiring efforts.

Artificial warmth is no longer required now and at last I can close down the heating system. The cost of oil is formidable and if prices continue to rise at the present rate I can foresee the time when perhaps only one house will be heated. At the same time, the few extra degrees of warmth during May nights considerably lengthen the season of tomatoes and flowering plants.

Mild June frosts normally do not present any problems, the warmth contained from daylight hours being sufficient to combat a drop in temperature at night. To be something of a weather prophet assists in the successful cultivation of a number of plants, none more so than tomatoes. Unfortunately, checked plants can be so handicapped that it takes many weeks for them to recover, and until the weather settles to warm nights and even warmer days it is vital to keep a sharp eye on ventilation as well as applying a lot of common sense to watering and feeding. As a general rule I try to water tomatoes in the early morning for the first half of the month and, if skies are clear, close down the windows in good time to retain heat.

I must not grumble, as the plants look well and carry three trusses of fruit on the early planting, while the pot-grown ones are not far behind. When compared, the two growing methods produce quite different plants. In pots the distance between leaf axils and fruit trusses is noticeably greater, leaves are narrower and not such a deep colour, stems are slightly thinner and uneven in girth. Open-ground plants are much closer jointed, lusher in foliage and stronger in the stem, and are without doubt the easiest to keep in vigorous growth throughout the season. My own observations, and I hope I am not biased because pot-grown toms need more attention, is that the ultimate crop varies little, but the flavour and texture of open-ground plants, whose root and feeding system are not contained, is definitely superior.

Looking back five years when heating was reasonably cheap, our minimum temperature was in the region of 13°C (55°F). In June we would be picking tomatoes, and the plant house was colourful and varied all the year round. With a tighter budget now the tomatoes are later but of better quality, flowering plants are less in number of species but are sturdier and longer lasting. Food for thought perhaps.

During my early days in horticulture I firmly believed the streptocarpus, or Cape primrose, was a plant of the hothouse and out of my grasp when I owned my first 2.5m × 2m (8ft × 6ft) wooden greenhouse. Modern breeding and a much closer look at the basic requirements of this beautiful flower has long since dispelled these thoughts. They are true perennials, lying almost dormant through the winter and needing only a minimal amount of water to prevent the central rosette of leaves from drying up. In spring, when new growth is made, careful division of the crown retaining pieces with fresh leaves showing will ensure plenty of stock for a summer and autumn display. Leaf cuttings also root readily and this is possibly the best method of increase to retain the hybrid vigour of a special plant.

To my mind, a smaller-flowered variety is the finest and this is Constant Nymph. The individual flowers are mid-blue fading to mauve and are produced on long well-branched stems held clear of the foliage. Starting this month they remain in flower until well into November, asking only for shade, a moist atmosphere and regular liquid feeding. They are excellent in the house too, as long as they receive an occasional overhead spray and continued feeding.

In their final 25cm (10in) clay pots, the stems of *Campanula pyramidalis* are beginning to lengthen. Having stood in frames since last September and formed large crowns under cool conditions they are now ready to be brought inside. Aptly named the chimney bell-flower, both the blue and white forms make magnificent specimen plants up to 2m (6ft) high; cane supports are needed as well as full sun until the flowers open. Up to this time ample watering and feeding is necessary and I normally limit the flowering spikes to six. I grow eight of these plants, four of each colour, housed in two batches – there is barely room for any more. As the flowers open feeding must be cut to a minimum, and some shade at this stage will prevent the blooms from fading. They also adapt to indoor conditions as long as they are light and airy. Standing in the large hall they make an imposing sight and are greatly admired by house guests. As long as the fading cups are nipped off to prevent seeding they will continue to flower for several weeks. Although seen at their best as a pot plant, they are also a decorative subject for warm corners and especially as a gap-filler at the back of a border.

The genus *Lilium* provides us with species and hybrids whose individual flowers are perhaps unsurpassed for beauty and colouring. I wish I could grow more of them in the garden, but frustratingly they barely tolerate our soil. Of course this does not mean we banish them completely; on the contrary, there are numerous varieties which will grow under alkaline or near neutral conditions. The field is considerably widened when they are grown as pot plants and their needs can be catered for. It is essential to purchase quality bulbs from a specialist supplier – beware of prepacked, dried-up offerings. Pot them as early as possible, preferably three to a 20cm (8in) pot in a compost that is perfectly drained and containing ample peat or coarse leafmould. Many varieties are stem rooting so leave space for topping up. Throughout their growth cycle they require no artificial heat; ours are stood in cold frames until April and then outside against a north-facing wall until flower buds appear. A central cane is all that is necessary for support, a task that should not be neglected as stems bent over by the wind seldom straighten again. Careful watering and a low-nitrogen fertiliser will keep growth sturdy.

Our first batch to be introduced under glass includes Enchantment, a vigorous grower with deep fiery-red blooms, and Fire King, deep orange with purple spots. Both these varieties are Asiatic hybrids of exceptional merit. As the first flowers open they are transferred to the manor house where their sweet heady fragrance drifts over many rooms.

Because of their almost tropical appearance, cannas (Indian shot plants) are extremely valuable for decoration purposes. There are many handsome varieties to choose from, with purple or green leaves and flowers ranging from pale pink and yellow to deep orange and red. A particular one that I am fond of is Lucifer, not so tall as

Fuchsias, Regal pelargoniums and cannas create a colourful corner in the plant house

most, with bright red flowers that are finely edged with yellow. They enjoy as much sunshine as possible and a very liberal supply of moisture combined with a twice-weekly feed. Roots with two or three growing crowns are potted into 20cm (8in) clay pots during March and kept as warm as possible until growth commences.

Amidst a colourful display in the plant house and while carrying on the daily task of watering and moving young plants to their final pots, it is again time to think about seed-sowing to ensure colour for next spring. Primulas and cinerarias are the mainstay, and sowings are made in early June and late July to provide a succession. Day temperatures under glass can often prove too high for both these subjects, and I prefer to use a shaded frame where possible. Primulas especially germinate better in suffused light and the cool airy conditions of a frame. On a hot June day temperatures can soar; I remember on one fateful occasion, when I had been occupied elsewhere in the garden, returning to the greenhouse only to find pans of frizzled-up seedlings.

The first time I took a specimen plant of *Rehmannia angulata* (Chinese foxglove) to the manor, it caused a great deal of speculation and admiration. Seldom seen outside private gardens, this half-hardy perennial is an excellent subject for the cool house in June, when the 1.2m (4ft) high stems are well furnished with pale pink

91

flowers not unlike an incarvillea. Seed-raised plants are superior to divisions; sown in July, the young plants need to be kept cool at all times and housed in a frost-free frame for the winter. Brought inside during March, they grow away rapidly and make fine plants.

The control of aphids is now of prime importance. Each house is fitted with electric generators, thermostatically controlled, that vaporise a range of insecticides. By far the most persistent is the whitefly which can raise certain problems in a mixed house. Prevention is always better than cure, and only by regular fumigation and spraying combined with glasshouse hygiene can this troublesome pest be eliminated. Smoke generators offer possibly the most efficient method of fumigation as long as temperatures are kept reasonably high, but immunity can quickly build up if one product only is used, so I find that changing occasionally to another brand can very often prove to be deadly.

Additional plants in flower this month are fuchsias, Regal pelargoniums, abutilons and celsias.

We all look forward to June, it is the first of the real growing months and the garden becomes alive with a great surge of leaf and flower. The lush growth of the bog garden is an outstanding feature: huge clumps of *Iris pseudacorus*, the yellow water flag, with its stately foliage are interplanted with forms of *Iris sibirica*, the bright blue Caesar being specially good – I like the way the tips of the narrow strap-like leaves bend gracefully over. Romping away in shallow water and over damp stones, *Mimulus luteus* is invasive but beautiful, the first flush of deep yellow musk flowers a sheer delight. It is also a voracious seeder and can become a nuisance in the moist pockets of the rock garden if not controlled.

That most noble of plants, *Gunnera manicata*, grows so well here in the fast running water of constant temperature that it occasionally dams the flow with its thick woody arms. Along with *Rheum palmatum*, whose 2.5m (8ft) high stems of deep rose 'rhubarb' flowers line the banks near the stone bridge, these giant foliaged plants create a tropical effect during summer.

The Candelabra group of hardy primulas have an extended flowering season and prefer some shade along with adequate moisture. Our new waterside bed is in full sun with a cool moist root-run, and already *Primula japonica* and *P. pulverulenta* are pushing up the first of their strong tiered stems.

Waterside planting of *Rheum palmatum*, the giant rhubarb

Opposite, on a moist shelving bank, clumps of *Aruncus sylvester* carry many handsome creamy white 1.2m (4ft) plumes. This so-called goat's beard is a favourite of mine, its attractive foliage and rather stately bearing making it an indispensable plant for good moist soil.

Many interesting plants are coming into flower on the rock garden, and try as one may to absorb the scene as a whole, it is completely dominated by *Genista lydia*, its arching and much-branched stems covered with the brightest of yellow flowers.

I find the dwarf aquilegias irresistible; some are not too long lived but most readily produce seed. Those diminutive little treasures *Aquilegia bertolonii* and *A. saximontana* both produce their flowers on 7.5cm (3in) stems and are quite at home in very well drained pockets that do not dry out. The *Linum* family provides us with some real gems. The bushy and rather tender *L. arboreum* has buttercup-yellow flowers over a long season with the added attraction of glaucous blue-green foliage; *L.* Gemmel's hybrid, of more dwarf habit and with large deep yellow flowers, is outstanding. Two other varieties I grow that are not so commonly seen are *L. capitatum* and *L. extra-axillare.* The former is similar in many ways to *L.* Gemmel's hybrid but is more vigorous and bears successive crops of yellow flaxen flowers well into early autumn. Just why *L. extra-axillare* is not more popular remains a mystery to me – its prostrate close-leaved stems produced in abundance terminate in charming sky-blue flowers.

Against a tall stone *Campanula barbata* makes a splendid show; I have a high regard for this plant – regretably not very long lived – which clothes its 23cm (9in) stems with soft blue bells whose lips are downed with soft hairs. Truly perennial is *C. carpatica* Turbinata which forms compact mats of deep purple-blue cups for many weeks, and Moonlight is equally free flowering with pale ice-blue saucers. Needing full sun in return for a long season of bloom is *Gypsophila repens* Dorothy Teacher, whose tiny pink flowers show up so well tumbling over a rock face.

In stony crevices *Erinus alpinus* Mrs Boyle and Dr Hanele create a wealth of colour with their pink and crimson flowers, modestly assuring us that they must rate highly in the world of alpines, seeding profusely but never a nuisance. These conditions also suit *Dianthus deltoides*, the maiden pink, whose forms include the deep wine Brilliant, the crimson Wisley variety, and Albus, a gem with pure white flowers and a deep pink eye.

Although the individual flowers of the dwarf bearded iris fade daily, this remains a fine plant for the large rock garden. Among the best varieties are Campbellii, which is deep violet, and the pale

Dianthus caryophyllus

yellow Moonlight. A moist pocket nearer the water is ideal for *Iris setosa* with its very attractive smoky-lilac, deeply veined flowers. On a sunny ledge moistened by tumbling water *Sisyrinchium macounii* Album will give its best. I never fail to admire this striking little plant, its short fans of quite broad leaves topped by very pure white flowers with a golden eye. Look for a well-drained, slightly shaded and moist spot, and plant it; it could well charm you for many summers.

Distinctive and with no fads, *Cotyledon simplifolia* (now generally called *Chiastophyllum oppositifolium*) should be more widely grown than it generally is. Clumps of succulent leaves remain close to the ground, whilst innumerable racemes of bright yellow grow in loops. Only 15cm (6in) high and preferring but not demanding a little shade, it benefits from replanting a little deeper every three years.

The end of the month sees many more plants in flower in the rock garden; among my favourites are *Anemone magellanica*, *Anemone narcissiflora*, the scented *Dianthus lemsii*, *Hypericum olympicum*, and *Erodium chamaedryoides* Roseum.

On a grassy bank running parallel to the bog garden we have a specimen tree of Japanese origin, *Magnolia obovata*. Seldom seen in gardens, it is completely tolerant of our stony land and, to my mind, is of considerable architectural merit. Our tree is well branched low

95

The unusual flat petals and crimson stamens of *Magnolia obovata*

down and protected from the worst of the wind by other trees. The flowers nestle over large and thick obovate leaves; from the petals, creamy white with the slightest tinge of pink in sunlight, rises a candle of claret-coloured stamens to be followed later by plum-coloured fruits. The fragrance is strong, especially in the early morning, and very reminiscent of thymol.

Nearby, and forming an effective contrast, stands a large *Buddleia alternifolia*. It is willow-leaved and of close arching habit, described by Farrer who also introduced it to this country, as a cascade of soft purple when in flower. Its fragrance attracts many insects and the old brittle growth beneath is home for many small birds.

Cherry blossom is over for another year, pink and white petals carpet the lawns, and one or two branches earmarked for removal earlier in the season are carefully sawn through and cuts painted over.

Often of untidy growth but invaluable for fragrance and, dare I say it, cutting, *Syringa vulgaris* or common lilac follows the *Prunus* family to bring a wealth of colour to many parts of the garden. Most are old trees, especially in the 'lilac walk' bordering the inner orchard, with varieties such as Souvenir de Louis Späth, Charles Joly and Madame Lemoine flowering freely on long misshapen branches. In the Maids Garden a white lilac showing blossom over the top of the wall is Maud Notcutt, without doubt the finest single white variety and possibly bearing the largest individual flowers of all. Of much smaller stature is the shrubby *S. palibiniana* (or *velutina*). A native of Korea, this choice species bears sprays of lilac-pink flowers deliciously scented, and its annual growth of just one or two centimetres makes it suitable for the large rock garden or shrub border. *S. microphylla*, of Chinese origin, is even neater producing miniature panicles of rosy lilac flowers.

As the main drive turns towards the dovecote two *Laburnum* × *watereri* Vossii are a fine sight with their long racemes of yellow flowers. This is perhaps not my favourite tree, though I must admit these are a spectacle when in full bloom.

Among a group of trees at the top of the church walk is *Cercis siliquastrum*, often referred to as the Judas tree. I must fault whoever planted it in this position, as it bears the brunt of biting north winds and is naturally reluctant to produce any quantity of the attractive purplish-pink pea flowers. Even so, the glaucous rounded leaves that follow are distinctive and finely coloured in the autumn, but what a pity a warmer spot was not selected for this good small tree.

Four viburnums flower this month, the best of which must be *Viburnum opulus* Sterile or snowball tree. It makes a wide bush, densely leaved and thickly covered with off-white, ball-shaped flowers. *V.o.* Compactum is a more dwarf version, seen at its best in the autumn when it carries bright scarlet fruit accentuated by golden leaves.

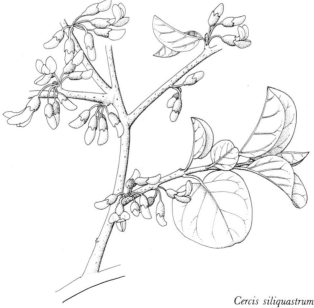

Cercis siliquastrum

Rather tender and needing wall protection is *V. japonicum* (*macrophyllum*), whose white flower heads, borne above deep glossy leaves, are very fragrant. One must be patient with this species as it is a shy flowerer until well established. A Chinese species, *V. rhytidophyllum*, is one of the noblest foliage plants I know. The cream flowers are of secondary importance compared with the heavily veined, evergreen leaves, narrow and up to 23cm (9in) long with a dense felting on the undersides. We have several large bushes up to 4.5m (15ft) in height facing mainly north against walls, and with their bonus of colourful berries in the autumn, these shrubs are of year-round attraction.

Down the main drive large trees of yew, cherry, *Prunus cerasifera* Pissardii and *Acer platanoides* Drummondii in particular, with leaves margined white, merge to show their foliage at their best.

Paeonies are unquestionably one of the loveliest plants for a June display. They revel in our limy conditions, asking only for an annual mulch of compost, and must be among the longest-lived perenials. In the pool garden a large warm border is devoted entirely to them, presenting us with a breathtaking drift of colour. The pink Sarah Bernhardt and the glowing carmine-red Felix Crousse are outstanding. I find no other flower can live with them, even if there were room, and apart from a walled background of climbing roses and clematis I am content to give them their freedom.

Paeony border with the gateway leading to the kitchen garden. Climbing roses on the wall include Zephirine Drouhin and Paul's Lemon Pillar

Looking through wrought iron gates to the courtyard. The centre-piece is an Italian well-head

Tree paeonies dislike our winds but on a sheltered wall of the pavilion, shaded by *Crataegus oxyacantha* Paul's Scarlet and (until recent years) *Ulmus glabra* Pendula, we have that magnificent variety *Paeonia lutea ludlowii*, its golden saucers sometimes 10cm (4in) across. Alas, the weeping elm has succumbed to Duch elm disease like all the other elms; it was a perfectly mushroomed specimen tree, so much a feature cascading down at the head of the pool, and will be missed by all.

In the borders the sword foliage of *Iris germanica* rises above all else. The individual flowers are charming and diversely coloured – I prefer the self shades such as those of Blue Rhythm, Ola Kala and Ramadin – yet the overall picture is rather short lived. On this well drained soil they increase at an alarming rate, and I feel that grouped together in an iris border would be the way of viewing them to their best advantage.

So diverse is the family *Geraniaceae*, excluding the greenhouse geranium, that there seldom exists a part of the garden where one or more species is not represented. Planted under trees or as a ground-coverer, in the borders or rock garden, their colour and long season of flowering make them indispensable. One of the most accommodating is *G. endressii*, bearing delicate pink flowers all

99

through the summer, and its hybrid Wargrave variety, slightly deeper and more compact, an excellent wall plant in sun or semi-shade. A good companion to both these varieties is *Geranium* Johnson's Blue with deeply cut foliage and masses of bright blue flowers well into autumn. The more upright *G. sylvaticum* Album is a fine border plant which associates well with delphinium or anchusa, and produces its pure white flowers by the hundred.

With a background of tall artemisia, *Euphorbia griffithii* Fireglow is a spectacular plant. Its orange-red bracts are quite startling, and for that I can forgive its annoying habit of spreading by underground stolons in all directions.

Tubs, urns and troughs on the terraces, in the courtyard and in places where extra colour is needed have been cleared of spring bulbs and flowers and await summer subjects. Some general fertiliser and a thorough soaking is necessary before they are planted up with zonal and ivy-leaved geraniums, trailing petunias and lobelia, *Helichrysum petiolatum* and fuchsias. All in all, they represent a great deal of work; in summer they need watering at least twice a week, dead-heading regularly and feeding with liquid manure in the height of the season. But on a summer's day, when the urns on the balustrading are a tumbling mass of pink and blue, it all seems worth it.

More interesting plants in flower this month are *Hebe glaucophylla, Alyssum serpyllifolium, Geranium ibericum, Iris tectorum* and *Erodium guttatum*. A tree-like shrub of great merit is *Cytisus battandieri* with lupin-like, pineapple-scented flowers. For sheer size the long sprays of white fragrant flowers on *Prunus padus* (the bird cherry) make this a handsome tree, though suitable only for the large garden.

JULY

Probably at no other time of the year is the plant house so well stocked and colourful, in fact I am almost spoilt for choice when selecting plants for decoration. It is hard to take one's attention away from the towering spikes of *Campanula pyramidalis*, now clothed for its entire length with wide open blue or white bells, spectacular plants whose beauty is enhanced by the warmth and protection of a greenhouse.

Not so impressive but equally as colourful are the fuchsias. In standard, bush and trailing form they have few equals for display, and their long season of flowering and great diversity of colour puts them in the top ten flowering plants for a cool house. I am very fond of standards, as seen at eye level the flower can be appreciated fully, and there is none better, I think, than Snowcap which makes a bushy head almost covered with contrasting red and white single blooms. Coachman, Dark Eyes and Display are all good in standard form, and the trailing Swingtime and La Campanella can be trained as small standards as well as cascading specimens.

Further lilies come into flower this month. They include *Lilium regale* and its hybrid form Royal Gold, and Green Dragon, another trumpet lily, white inside with conspicuous yellow stamens and a cool chartreuse-green on the outside. All are superb varieties filling the plant house with their strong fragrance.

I have never had any great liking for the white arum lily, *Richardia* (*Zantedeschia*) *aethiopica*, but two other species I find charming. *R. elliottiana* has well-shaped, deep yellow flowers shown up to great advantage by its dark shiny leaves mottled with white. Even more attractive is *R. rehmannii*, a more dwarf, narrow-foliaged form with pale shell-pink flowers. Both are happy in pots as long as the soil is rich and fibrous, and they need placing in the warmest part of the house.

It's true that some people can take an instant dislike to a certain plant. Amongst various bulbous subjects I grow is the ismene, a plant from the Andes bearing pure white flowers with spidery

The pavilion at the head of the pool garden

reflexed segments. I quite like it, although admittedly it has a strange insectivorous appearance, despite its common name of Peruvian daffodil. I remember the day well when I took down a nicely flowered plant to the manor, only to be asked to remove it!

Two other good bulbous subjects in flower now are *Eucomis bicolor* with its unusual green and lilac stars in the form of a pineapple, and *Haemanthus kalbreyeri* which bears a large umbel of orange-scarlet flowers with prominent stamens.

I have long admired the large delicate blooms of the tuberous begonia, but because of their intolerance to being moved I have in recent years relied more on the fibrous-rooted species. One exception is the multiflora type bearing numerous small flowers on compact plants, whose free flowering habit makes it an admirable subject. From varieties generally available I would select Mrs Richard Galle, coppery yellow, and the soft yellow Mrs. Helen Harms. The fibrous rooted species, however, given shade and a moist atmosphere, are plants of great charm. *Begonia sutherlandii*, which is a *gracilis* type, I have already praised; its red-stemmed orange flowers over graceful foliage captivate all who see or grow it. *B. fuchsioides*, which can reach 1m (3ft) or more, is of an upright spreading habit and bears clusters of deep pink flowers at each leaf joint, and whilst *B. mettalica* does produce pale pink flowers its beauty lies in the sheen and metallic tints of its foliage. Also in this category is *B. rex*, grown for its huge leaves of contrasting zoned colours. It is perfectly happy growing under the staging.

A plant I grow as *B.* Lucerna, correctly named or not, can reach 2m (6ft) or more and makes a marvellous focal specimen. Its stems are mahogany brown and strongly branched, new leaf sheaths are crimson and from them develop the large olive-green leaves, often with a fine white mottling near the stem. The reverse of the leaves is a rich ruby red and heavily veined, making this plant worthy of merit on foliage alone. Even so, it bears panicles of soft pink flowers throughout the summer and into late autumn, the sheer weight of bloom making it necessary to provide support for the somewhat brittle stems.

All these species need a fibrous, rather acidic soil and should not be allowed to dry out completely during the winter.

Coming into flower is an annual of particular attraction, *Torenia fournieri.* Its deep purple and mauve flowers have an orchid-like appearance and are always admired by visitors. As it needs only some shade and cool moist surroundings I often wonder why it is not more widely grown.

In the sunny half of the house, cannas steal the show and need abundant watering and feeding to keep them in first-class condition. Neglect of either of these duties will lead to an immediate halt in flower production.

All three varieties of *Campanula isophylla* are bursting into flower and form a magnificent edging along the benches. They are so adaptable too – perhaps at their best when allowed to tumble freely from a hanging basket, but also an excellent subject for all-round decoration. Not quite so vigorous but equally splendid is *C. fragilis.* Strictly speaking it is an alpine plant not taking kindly to our wet winters, but under glass it showers its trailing stems with masses of porcelain-blue saucers. Easily raised from seed or division in spring, it is a little gem.

Breeders continue to present us with a bewildering number of varieties of impatiens, many at bewildering prices, yet I must admit it is a vastly improved plant compared with the Busy Lizzie of years gone by. They are excellent for bedding out and even better as pot plants, flowering for months on end and extremely valuable as either a single specimen or as a base filler for tall subjects. Seed is expensive and should be handled carefully, and on no account should early raising be attempted unless conditions are right, when germination is rapid. A moist atmosphere and a minimum bottom heat of 18°C (65°F) is essential, after which slightly cooler temperatures will suit. They seem to prefer pot-bound conditions so don't over-pot in the early stages and keep to a 12.5cm (5in) pot for the final move. When they are in flower, weekly liquid feed is important as well as removal of fading flowers. By extending seed-sowing over the spring months it is possible to have these decorative plants in flower until Christmas. My own choice is the FI Zig Zag strain, with many shades of pink and scarlet on a white background. Copious supplies of water and light shade are greatly appreciated.

No July display is complete without the gloxinia, one of the most handsome tuberous-rooted plants. Its velvety leaves provide an excellent foil to the wide smooth trumpets of which thirty or more can be produced on a single plant. From February sowings, if the temperature can be maintained at 18°C (65°F), strong young plants can be raised for late summer flowering. Unfortunately this is beyond our range and I have to rely on corms started into growth during March and kept in the warmest place possible. During the whole period of growth the compost must be a fine peaty one with plenty of sand to assist drainage. Water sparingly, keeping the soil just slightly damp to the touch, and on no account allow any quantity on the foliage. Gloxinias benefit most by a moist atmosphere and surroundings; shade from strong sunshine is also necessary, and liquid feeding should commence once the buds swell up. As house plants they are reasonably tolerant as long as the air is not too dry.

Tomatoes are ripening well and we have been picking since the first week of this month. It is a head gardener's privilege to sample the very first fruit, after which I am greeted with a smile from the cook when a kilo or two are presented to the kitchen. I hope she appreciates the hard work that goes into growing them.

To keep up a regular supply of fruit as well as maintaining the plants in healthy growth requires time and a considerable understanding of what I term a complex plant. Foremost, I'm sure, are ventilation and the growing atmosphere, but with our ample side and top ventilators it is relatively easy to keep the day temperature around the 18°–21°C (65°–70°F) mark. Tomatoes like plenty of fresh air but not draughts, a buoyant atmosphere (ie containing a degree of moisture) for some hours of the day, but not constant humidity. Watering, also, is a key factor. A fast-growing plant needs at least 2 litres (4pt) on a sunny day but, perhaps more important, the fine drinking roots should never at any time be allowed to go dry. Our open bed presents few problems, but the plants in pots are quick to show their dislike of any disorder in watering or feeding. In fact they need a rather different approach, and a common mistake I regularly see is over-feeding leading to a salt concentration.

A good crop of tomato FI hybrid MM in clay pots and a loam based compost

The tomato makes tremendous demands on the growing media, and it has always been my firm policy to work out a feeding programme in the early season and stick to it rigidly. The roles played by nitrogen and potash are vital; from the preparation of the bed and mixing of the potting soil they are, in my opinion, the most important single factor, right through the season to the last picking on an autumn day.

Further sowings of all groups of primulas, as well as cinerarias, are made during the month, and again the shaded frame offers the best conditions. An excellent strain of cinerarias that produces compact plants in a wide colour range is Spring Glory, or if room is available the larger *hybrida grandiflora* make superb specimens. The seldom grown Stellata type can also be raised now.

A great favourite of the Victorian era was the calceolaria, and although it lost popularity for a number of years I am glad to say that, mainly due to the modern multiflora type, it is once again being widely grown. A sowing now will provide flowering plants for next spring, and at no time during its life does it require any but cool conditions. *Browallia speciosa major*, winter stock, mignonette, *Celsia arcturus* and *Trachelium coeruleum* can all be sown too for spring colour.

This is an ideal time to increase stock of herbaceous and alpine plants by soft tip cuttings. These are taken preferably in the early

105

morning, inserted into a fine sandy mixture and placed in a propagating frame that can support a moist close atmosphere. Dwarf shrubs such as hebes and potentillas also strike well now, enabling them to make well-rooted plants before winter.

Many subjects that prefer the cooler air are stood outside for the summer months. They include amaryllis, jasmine, ismene and solanum, and both *Azalea indica* and *Cymbidium* orchids are equally happy against a north-facing wall or hedge. Clivias, too, enjoy a few weeks of abundant fresh air in a sheltered position, as long as feeding and watering are not neglected.

Other additions in the plant house are *Hoya carnosa*, achimenes in variety, coleus, fragrant geraniums and salpiglossis.

The delicate wax-like flowers of *Hoya carnosa*, an evergreen climber in the plant house

It is in the month of July that the kitchen garden displays its highly individual design to the full. Trained pears stand neat and fruitful along the perimeter walls, standard apple trees line the well mown grass reservations, long straight rows of vegetables in various stages of growth stretch across the growing areas. The picture as a whole reflects the hard work of all concerned.

An abundance of soft fruit and vegetables makes necessary a concentrated effort of picking until at least mid-morning every day. The early strawberries are almost finished and the protective netting is removed so that we can control the weed seedlings that inevitably come from strawing. To follow on we have the mid-season Red Gauntlet, a heavy cropper especially on two- and three-year-old plants. It carries fruit well above the foliage on strong stems and does not need strawing. The fruit is large and well shouldered, or lumpy as we call it, and of delicious flavour. Although birds have lost a little of their initial interest, this later crop still requires netting, as they continue the annoying habit of pecking one small hole in each fruit, given the chance. Choice of variety is very much dependent on what suits a particular soil; many gardens cannot grow Royal Sovereign due to virus infection, but here it is virus free. The third variety of Strawberry was already a resident when I started work here, and comes as near to perpetual fruiting as I have seen; runners are produced in all directions and they, too, bear fruit during late summer. The variety could be Ghento, but I am not sure. The fruit is rather ugly and ripens spasmodically, but I retain a few plants each year for its ability to produce late fruit.

Runners can now be used as a means of increasing or replacing stock. It is of utmost importance that only healthy and virus-free plants are used for this purpose. By far the most practical method is to layer selected runners direct into 7.5cm (3in) pots of good soil, avoiding root disturbance later when transplanting them to their permanent home. The added advantage of making a start early this month is that the new plants could well bear fruit the following year.

The warmer, more humid nights, greatly assist the ripening of raspberries, the first of which we are picking now. Our earliest variety is Malling Exploit, which has large crops of medium-sized fruits of fine flavour. Following on later in the month is Malling Jewel, a variety that insists on a rich soil and plenty of moisture. It is a little shy in producing new canes, yet in my estimation it is the best flavoured raspberry of all.

I know only too well that once raspberries appear at the kitchen, strawberries are quickly out of favour, giving me time to put a quantity in the freezer and allowing me to sell the remainder to eager buyers. This is not the case with the small alpine strawberries, which are always constantly in demand. A long single row bordering one of the grass paths is just starting to fruit and will continue to do so for many weeks. Their flavour is quite unique and they need to be left on the plant until they are fully ripe. Picking is very time-consuming, and a costing of a punnetful would be startling to say the least, but who would be without them?

As Careless gooseberries are all picked, the slightly later Leveller begins to ripen. This is a most reliable variety with juicy yellow fruit, standing well in good condition for some time. Many will go to the kitchen for crumbles and jam making, but a large proportion will be frozen, keeping so well as they do and providing a tasty addition for the winter months. We also grow a few plants of Whinhams Industry, the last gooseberry to ripen to its deep red colour, but of excellent sweet flavour. Needing some care when pruning, this variety, like Leveller, will only produce quality fruit on land that is in good heart.

The picking of blackcurrants is also a tedious job, especially when so much other work is pressing. Unless a sudden glut of this fruit is needed it is as well to spread out the time of maturity over a number of weeks. We do this by growing early, mid-season and late varieties, namely Boskoop Giant, Wellington XXX and Baldwin. Condition of the currants when picking is very important and a daily check is necessary to prevent over-ripening.

Both red and white currants present no real difficulties, except for attacks by marauding birds who have a great liking for the white. Again we freeze a large percentage of the crop.

Planted only two years ago, a run of loganberry LY 59 bears a good crop of fruit, and by the end of the month a few of its delicious dark red berries should be ripe. It is an extremely vigorous variety requiring careful pruning and tying in if a tangled mass of thorny stems is to be avoided. The new canes that are generously produced must also be controlled or picking can be made difficult. A top dressing of fertiliser in early spring and a mulch of well rotted compost during May will go a long way towards preserving moisture and extending the fruiting season.

Broad beans continue to crop prolifically; try as one may to, carry their season over a number of weeks, it seems inevitable that by the end of July there are almost too many to cope with. Young pods of small tender beans go to the kitchen, the surplus of this size are put in the freezer. Blackfly can so often infest the succulent tips of the leaves and control is necessary to prevent them spreading elsewhere. Where possible, I use an organic spray based on vegetable oils and extracts, it is non-poisonous and just as effective as many chemical products. As picking is completed the plants are cut to the ground but the roots left in. They contain nitrogen, proof of which can be plainly seen, as land that previously grew legumes and was subsequently put down to ryegrass clearly showed improved colour and as much as 10cm (4in) of extra growth where the rows were originally sited.

July in particular has several firsts, none so eagerly waited for as the first early peas. We have a fine row of Kelvedon Wonder, ideally suited to our land and a heavy cropper of excellent flavour. A round-

(*Left*) John and Stuart picking early pea Kelvedon Wonder. (*Right*) John lifts the first root of early potatoes, in this case Pentland Javelin

seeded type would perhaps be a fortnight earlier, but I find them rather flavourless and much prefer to wait for the sweet wrinkled varieties. A basket of fresh pods still with the early morning dew on them is truly a fine sight, and their popularity in the kitchen is such that there is a marked decrease in the demand for other vegetables when they appear. This is one crop that we do not irrigate unless the plants show definite signs of wilting; the preparation of the ground and organic content are really the key factors. All our rows are sticked – we are fortunate there is no shortage of good hazel to provide ample support. Following on from Kelvedon Wonder we have Progress No 9 with larger, more pointed pods and, again, of excellent flavour.

The season for sowing peas is almost over, but I revert to an early variety and make one final row. Whether they will mature in the autumn is something of a gamble. Weather conditions are the deciding factor, but occasionally the gamble pays off.

At last we are able to pull the first young carrots from unthinned rows, the time between the last of the winter ones and the present crop being longer than usual due to the cold wet spring. New potatoes also are now being lifted, with Pentland Javelin easily the first to produce our early crop, eagerly waited for by all. Everything good now seems to come at once.

Less glamorous, perhaps, but always a good standby are the summer cabbages. Since its introduction I have found none better than June Star, whose tight round heads without a scrap of waste remain in good condition for several weeks. As so often is the case we have a few too many cauliflowers maturing together, but if the curds are cut in prime condition they will freeze successfully. Lettuce Avoncrisp, Little Gem and Tom Thumb are cut daily along with radish Rota and French Breakfast, and fine young spring onions.

By the end of the month we are picking dwarf beans The Prince, a daily task if the young almost stringless pods are to be had at their best. The runner beans are also making strong growth now as their roots find moisture.

Japanese onions have been a great success this season. Express Yellow, an FI hybrid, has produced a row of medium-sized bulbs with very little splitting or bolting, and coming into maturity as they do now, this type admirably fills the gap until maincrop onions are lifted.

After a night's rain young plants of purple and white sprouting broccoli, cabbage Minicole, January King and Bartolo, and lettuce Continuity are lined out. Seeds sown are carrot Autumn King, perpetual spinach beet, beetroot Boltardy, spring cabbage Flower of Spring and First Early Market, and salad crops. From now on lettuce is drilled direct and thinned to 40cm (15in) apart, minimising the tendency to bolt.

In recent years herbs have again become very popular. Apart from parsley which is needed every day in summer, we have a permanent bed for sage, thyme, chives and scallions, to which we have added marjoram, tarragon and rosemary.

During the last half century, the herbaceous perennial has been in and out of fashion more times than I care to mention, but now it is enjoying a well-deserved popularity. Much credit can go to the breeders for introducing greatly improved qualities in many varieties which indirectly reduce maintenance. The herbaceous border, or the more modern concept of the island bed, truly typifies the image of a country garden. No other group of plants can provide a three-month or longer display of brilliant colour and variety.

The plants I mention or describe in the following chapters are but a few of the many we have introduced to this garden in the last six years. Some are personal favourites, while others possess out-standing qualities.

Already established when I arrived here, *Alstroemeria ligtu* hybrids are amongst the first and most beautiful plants that flower this month. Often slow to establish themselves in anything but the right conditions, which are as much sunshine as possible and a moist but

Cabbage lettuce Webbs Wonderful
and cos lettuce Lobjoits Green

Alstroemeria ligtu hybrid requires full
sun and a deep root run

well-drained root-run, they will reward care and patience with fine heads of cream, pink, salmon and orange flowers on strong stems ideal for cutting.

For sheer volume of flower over many weeks, penstemons can seldom be matched. This is a plant that I will always grow although it is of doubtful hardiness, surviving only mild winters. *Penstemon* Garnet is probably the hardiest, often losing top growth only to show fresh new buds in late spring. It is not uncommon to see its carmine-red flower spikes for five months of the year. *P.* Ruby is a delightful claret shade and vigorous, *P.* Evelyn has a much more dwarf habit with deep pink flowers, but one of the most charming varieties, though regrettably rather tender, is *P.* Blue Springs, bearing small spikes of azure blue. To make sure that stock is available each year, soft cuttings should be rooted this month and over-wintered in a frame.

Two varieties of *Crocosmia* that we have tried, Lucifer and Spitfire, have more than lived up to our expectations. The 1m (3ft) wiry stems of *C.* Lucifer carry sprays of flame-red flowers over broad sword-like leaves, while *C.* Spitfire is only slightly smaller at just over 60cm (2ft) and has deep orange flowers. Both seem hardy and are an extremely attractive addition to the mixed border.

As I have studied the family Campanulaceae for many years, it seems only natural that they should be well represented in our garden. *Campanula lactiflora* Pritchard's Variety is without doubt a superb plant with its huge trusses of violet blue cups on 1.2m (4ft) stems that are so freely produced, and often bearing a second crop of flowers in late summer. *C. l.* Loddon Anna is a distinct colour break with soft lilac-pink flowers on tall stems, seen at their best in light shade and not too dry a position. Both these cultivars need a rich soil to live up to the Award of Merit and Award of Garden Merit that they deservedly received. The deep violet *C. glomerata* Superba is another fine form which needs regular division to keep the flowers large and plentiful, the same conditions also suiting *C. persicifolia* Telham Beauty with its deep china-blue saucers.

An indispensable back-row perennial that remains in flower for most of the summer is the anchusa. A difficult plant to stake, it is, I find, better given plenty of room and allowed to ramble. The gentian-blue Morning Glory is a striking form, and Loddon Royalist is an even deeper colour. Anchusas dislike winter wet, which often kills the main thong, but fortunately the smaller roots usually survive and grow. Good forms can also be raised from seed.

Good 'blues' are so valuable in the border that I would hate to be without delphiniums. We have numerous good named varieties, and almost as good seed-raised ones, but regrettably all suffer from the ever-present strong winds. It is for this reason that we now concentrate on plants that do not exceed 1.5m (5ft) and this applies not only to delphiniums but to other varieties also. Especially colourful just now are *Sidalcea* Rose Queen, *Aquilegia* Celestial Blue, *Lychnis chalcedonica*, *Anthemis* Mrs Buxton and *Geranium armenum*. Two centaureas or perennial cornflowers that are particularly interesting both in foliage and flower are *Centaurea pulchra major* with grey jagged leaves and pink flowers, and *C. ruthenica*, which has glossy laciniated foliage and sulphur-yellow flowers.

Although its flowers do not appear until late August, *Sedum maximum* Atropurpureum is a foliage plant of great effect. However, the purple-red succulent leaves can very often be badly marked with heavy rain, in fact the plant itself needs careful placing. By accident, I found it combined very well with *Perovskia* Blue Spire, a shrub with grey foliage on white mealy stems, topped with slender spikes of lavender-blue flowers.

Providing flower from now until October, the potentillas are among the finest dwarf shrubs available. One of their virtues is that they will grow almost anywhere except deep shade or waterlogged ground. They vary from choice alpine species barely 2.5cm (1in) high to dense shrubs up to 1.5m (5ft). Personally, I think they enjoy light shade for some of the day and possibly a lower pH than we

Geranium armenum – a colourful herbaceous plant

have; nevertheless they grow very successfully here and our limy soil does much to accentuate flower colour. Our tallest, and incidentally the earliest variety, is Katherine Dykes, perpetually covered with primrose-yellow flowers; an old specimen near the head of the rock garden blooms for months on end. *Potentilla* Jackman's Variety, slightly less tall at 1.2m (4ft), has deep yellow flowers that are particularly long lasting and combine well with the grey-green foliage. *P. fruticosa* Farreri is a neat grower with many quite small bright yellow flowers over tiny narrow leaves. If I had to choose just one variety, and thank goodness I don't, it would have to be *P. fruticosa* Elizabeth, initially a rather untidy grower but eventually making a dome-shaped bush 60cm (2ft) high studded with large, pale yellow flowers. Leaves are grey with just a hint of green, and here they associate well with *Ruta* Jackman's Blue and *Sedum* Ruby Glow.

Potentilla fruticosa

Although this family is predominantly yellow flowered there are a few hybrids with a distinct colour break. Both the cream and apricot Daydawn and the orange Sunset are first-class varieties, suitable in the mixed shrubbery or neat enough for the large rockery, preferring light shade to prevent their pastel colours from 'yellowing'

The silver-grey leaves and yellow daisies of *Senecio greyi* blend perfectly with the Cotswold stone, I think it is underrated as a shrub creating excellent background colour for smaller highly coloured subjects. Needing only full sun and a dry stony soil, it can be loosely

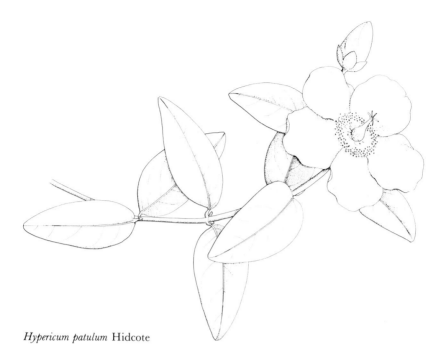

Hypericum patulum Hidcote

termed an evergreen, although here it is often defoliated by severe frost, only to burst into life again in spring.

We have several deutzias about the garden, easily cultivated but not really colourful, with the exception of two cultivars. The carmine-pink flowers of *D. compacta* Rosealind have a certain charm during May, but by far the best one is *D. pulchra*. A native of Taiwan, it bears long racemes of pure white flowers, each spike gracefully arching over to give an effect similar to drooping lily-of-the-valley. In the Maids' Garden there is a 2.1m (7ft) high specimen of this variety, and what a picture it is this month!

Another shrub that gives us great service in many different situations is *Hypericum patulum* Hidcote. Probably the hardiest of the species, it is valuable as a ground-coverer or as a dwarf hedge and merits space as a single specimen. It will reach nearly 2m (6ft) in height, but I prefer to prune it hard every other year, keeping it bushy and thus producing many of the buttercup-yellow flowers each with a pale ring of stamens. A truly magnificent form in this family is *H.* × Rowallane. It demands a warm south-facing wall, where it sometimes reaches 2.5m (8ft), and the huge bowl-shaped flowers, as much as 7.5cm (3in) across, are delicately moulded. I have lost many specimens, but continue to plant it, such is the beauty of this shrub.

I would like to grow more escallonias, but they are not a plant for these parts. The one variety I do grow is the perfectly hardy *Escallonia* Gwendolyn Anley, its spreading bushy habit never invasive, and the pale pink flowers remaining with us all summer.

In the rock garden many summer-flowering alpines are at their best. Dwarf campanulas temporarily dominate the scene with varieties including *Campanula carpatica* Bressingham White, Chewton Joy and Isobel, a fine deep blue form with flat saucers that seem to look up at you. For number and succession of flower *C. innesii* is a fine variety; rarely seen in gardens now, it is well worth growing for its light blue bells. Wandering about under moist stones and on gritty ledges are the tiny grey-blue *C.* Miss Wilmott and the even more diminutive *C.* × *hallii* with its white bells. A favourite of mine is *C.* Lynchmere, of upright habit and with delightful deep violet cups all the way up 20cm (8in) stems.

A recently introduced *Platycodon* from Japan is *P. grandiflorus* Apoyama, whose 15cm (6in) stems carry numerous ballooned buds that open into lavender-blue flowers veined purple. We have several clumps of this beautiful dwarf species, and it is advisable to mark their positions as the dormant thongs are easily damaged during winter.

Symphandra hofmanii

A snow-white *rugosa* rose, Blanc de Coubert, a highly scented and continuous flowering variety

A host of other colourful plants include *Dianthus* Pikes Pink, *D.* Dubarry, *Erodium macradenum, Geranium* Ballerina, *Potentilla eriocarpa* and *Veronica rupestris.* The many colourful forms of the *Helianthemum,* or rock rose, are excellent for dry slopes or when allowed to cascade over broad rock faces. The primrose-yellow *H.* Wisley Primrose is certainly one of the best and not over-vigorous, while, if space is limited, the delightful *H. lunulatum* should be grown.

Aside from trees and shrubs, herbaceous plants and alpines, it is the routine maintenance that keeps the garden looking lovely. Grass-cutting alone is a full-time job for one man, while there is a multitude of hoeing and dead-heading, tying in and watering and, very soon, hedge-cutting. To myself and my staff it is immensely enjoyable, though hard work, but when at the end of a day we can look across a tree-shaded lawn to colourful borders and hear the music of running water, it all seems very worthwhile.

AUGUST

As temperatures soar on sunny days, the moisture needs of individual plants under glass are of prime importance. Moisture-loss can be deceivingly rapid and is not necessarily visual; it is only by experience and a thorough knowledge of each plant's requirements that the contents of the greenhouse can be maintained in first-class condition. Just when to water can often depend on other commitments in the garden – in some cases plants will need water twice a day. As a professional gardener I arrange my time to suit the plants, and this month especially I prefer to work in the early evening when the sun loses its fierceness and inside temperatures drop to a more workable level.

Damping down the central paths as well as the benching gravel in the early mornings, and afternoons also on the hottest days, is an important routine task, and considerably helps to create a level of humidity which is extremely beneficial to most subjects.

The variation in potting composts can be a deciding factor when watering; a soil-less compost, or a mixture containing 40 per cent loam such as we use for acid-loving plants, holds considerable amounts of water over a long period, but if allowed to dry out will present real problems. Our basic compost of seven parts loam, four parts peat and three parts grit and sand by bulk, needs frequent but less copious waterings. The two types of mixture also require two different approaches in regard to feeding: generally speaking, a low percentage loam mixture will need more frequent feeding, as nutrients are not held in for any length of time.

By no means do I condemn the introduction of the plastic pot; cheap, hygienic and easily cleaned, they are here to stay for a few years yet. Clay pots, on the other hand, are expensive and scarce, but having a large stock come down to us from earlier days we naturally use them on many occasions. For taller plants and those with branching stems heavy with flower, they are essential. The roots of certain plants – fuchsias I think are one example – shy away from non-absorbent plastic.

A summer scene on the east terrace, the unrestricted growth softening the contours of the stonework

The two types of pot also require different methods of watering. With clay, the moisture content can be checked with a 'pot-tapper' – ours is a bamboo cane attached to a wooden bobbin. A mellow ring indicates water is needed, a dull thud means the pot contains sufficient moisture. Such refined methods cannot be applied to plastic pots; here one has to resort to weight for some help, but in both cases the colour of the soil can help the experienced eye to make a fairly accurate assessment.

Aphids can be troublesome this month if not rigorously controlled. Smokes and vaporisers are very thorough as long as temperatures are around the 18°C (65°F) mark, and I like to make sure they have done their job by checking the undersides of leaves of plants I know are renowned harbourers, namely fuchsias, browallias and tomatoes.

Primulas, cinerarias and calceolarias that germinated in the cold frame last month are ready for a move. As yet they are not sizeable enough for potting, but like many other plants they benefit greatly from a move at this stage and I transfer them to trays. The roots are fine and need a sandy soil to develop further. They are returned to the frame where they must be shaded and kept evenly moist.

Apart from foliage plants, the only seeds I sow now are

119

schizanthus and browallia. Schizanthus germinate very quickly and must be potted at a very young stage. Kept in a frame until September they will develop into sturdy plants for flowering next spring. Many different strains are available including the giant pansy-flowered mixture that makes huge specimen plants. My own choice is the more compact but very colourful Hit Parade. Browallias are merely a gamble, as weather conditions will determine whether they flower for Christmas or not. A sowing now of a *semperflorens* begonia can often produce interesting results.

Inside the plant house there is a very colourful display, with so many subjects at the peak of their flowering – cannas, impatiens, campanulas and fuchsias, along with gloxinias, trachelium and begonias. The scabious-like blue flowers of *Didiscus caeruleus* are something a little different, and although it is a half-hardy annual this charming plant is enhanced to the full under glass.

Another very attractive pot plant is *Microsperma* Golden Tassel, which has pale green primula foliage above which many lemon-yellow hypericum-like flowers are borne, the very prominent stamens adding considerably to the charm of this species.

Coleus, now in 15cm (6in) pots, make a wonderful foliage display and need the insignificant flower spikes nipping out to keep them growing. As well as the straight-leaved varieties, I grow the Sabre mixture, a distinct strain with long pointed leaves and self-branching habit, ideally suited for smaller pots.

Achimenes have always been great favourites of mine, adapting themselves to pot or basket culture in their upright or trailing forms. Flowers are very freely produced, diverse in colour and long lasting. They must have shade and a degree of humidity, ample water when growing strongly, and weekly applications of liquid feed. An open, fibrous compost suits them – equal parts loam, leafmould, peat and sand I find most suitable – and five tubers to a 11cm (4½in) pot will give a glorious effect. Varieties are countless, my own preference going to Camille Brozzoni with white-eyed lilac flowers in great profusion, the deep pink Peach Blossom, Shirley Fireglow, an outstanding orange-scarlet variety, and Little Beauty whose pure pink blooms have a yellow eye. There are many more, all desirable.

The shrimp plant, *Beloperone guttata*, aptly named with reference to its red bracts and white flowers, is well suited to greenhouse or home conditions. The bulk of its flowers are produced in midsummer, but except in the coldest months this accommodating plant will flower almost endlessly. It needs re-potting annually in early spring, and over a number of years will make a handsome bush. Propagation is by cuttings any time in summer, brought on in a closed frame.

Acidanthera bicolor murielae

For fragrance, *Acidanthera bicolor murielae* has few equals. This is a bulbous plant from Ethiopia, and revels in the extra warmth of a glasshouse. The flowers are large white stars with a purple-maroon blotch, borne on slender arching stems over broad leaves. In the garden it blooms in late September, but not being fully hardy it is best lifted for the winter.

A number of foliage plants can be raised from seed; most need high temperatures for germination, and this month provides just this. They include *Schefflera digitata* and *S. arboricola, Dracaena indivisa* (tie palm), *Aralia sieboldii* and *Nandina domestica*, the latter having scarlet tints on the young leaves. All will tolerate much lower temperatures after germination.

A few other plants adding to the overall display are *Lilium speciosum* Grand Commander, *Asparagus meyerii, Plectranthus coleoides* Marginata, and *Hoya carnosa.*

Tomatoes are at the height of their productive season and require picking daily. The adequate side ventilation, a feature of all our glasshouses, can now be fully appreciated, and by planning a current of cool air between them and the roof vents it is possible to maintain a healthy growing atmosphere. Very few plants require temperatures in excess of $18°-21°C$ ($65°-70°F$), many will visually show their dislike and watering becomes a full time job. Curled leaves on tomato plants are often wrongly diagnosed as some form of virus, whereas in most cases it is the combination of high daytime and low night temperatures, resulting in poor fruit setting and elongated truss formation.

As a rule during this month, I reduce the ratio of potash slightly and increase the nitrogen in our liquid feed. So often the reserves of nitrogen are played out, and this stepping up will encourage active growth into the early autumn months.

After last month's hectic soft fruit season we are still able to pick some late raspberries. Some people would find the colour of the yellow-fruited Golden Everest slightly off-putting, but we find it a very valuable addition. The berries are of a mild sweet flavour often shyly produced on both old and young canes. Norfolk Giant, on the other hand, is extremely tall and vigorous, canes are freely made and some limitation is necessary if quality is more important than quantity. The fruit is firm and highly coloured, and with its sharp acid flavour makes superb jam.

Loganberries are ripening to a dull red colour. I adore this sharp-flavoured fruit that must be left on the cane until fully ripe, a welcome addition in the kitchen and the instigator of many culinary pleasures.

French beans are continually prductive but are now put in the shade by the first of the runner beans Achievement. This variety is a selection from Streamline, and produces fine pods in bunches over a long period. Again it is quality I look for. Having grown many of the old favourites such as Prizewinner and Scarlet Emperor that have stood the test of time, I think Achievement has just an edge in texture. The pods must be picked young and tender, preferably before sun-up. This is one crop that must never suffer from lack of moisture, as failure to irrigate thoroughly in dry spells can lead to a drastic check in growth and flower.

This also applies to celery and celeriac in particular, in fact in times of no rainfall many crops will greatly benefit from a drenching applied as a fine spray. The exception are peas. They love a sharp shower or even persistent drizzle, but try as one may to simulate these conditions with a sprinkler they quickly discolour and sprawl.

There are plenty of good carrots at last, Early Nantes and Amsterdam Forcing, as well as golf ball sized beetroot Boltardy, radish, spring onion and lettuce, the best hearts coming from Continuity, Avoncrisp and Lobjoits Green cos.

Broad beans have almost finished, and early peas are cleared and the ground cleaned – they seem to harbour more than their fair share of weeds. Greenshaft peas continue to bear well in succession and, along with runner beans, need daily attention.

The bed of maincrop onions looks well and they are enjoying sunny days to the full. Careful hoeing is necessary between the rows to prevent any damage to the swelling bulbs. The quality seed-raised varieties are showing an inclination to bend their leaves, and to help them ripen we turn over the tops. The Japanese type continue to supply the kitchen and it is time to sow for next year. Much is talked and written about these onions, most of which is over-technical and could well deter an amateur from trying this valuable crop. In my own opinion, the sowing time is crucial; here it is the third week of this month and the seed bed is prepared in advance accordingly. It was generally accepted at one time that transplanting led to as much as 25 per cent loss in winter, but I beg to differ on this point. We move ours to really well firmed ground as soon as the plants are size-able, and out of last season's 120 plants we lost only two, proving beyond doubt that, with care, they will adapt themselves to normal onion-growing procedures.

Now that strawberries are over for another year all old stems and foliage are removed close to the ground, and rooted layers in pots are severed from the parent plant and stood in an open frame to thicken up before planting in the permanent bed. Each year, crowns that have completed their third season are dug up, and the ground is rested for twelve months.

Alpine strawberries, of which we have an abundance just now, are treated similarly, and fresh stocks are raised from seed every three years. If the ground becomes dry it is essential to irrigate, as a lack of moisture for any length of time seriously curtails cropping, and berries become dry and seedy.

An inspection of all early potatoes indicates the beginning of slug damage, not unexpected considering the wet conditions of late spring. The crop is lifted, some placed in hessian sacks for immediate use, the remainder stored in dry straw in an airy stable. Sutton's Foremost, although not among the harbingers of earlies, is one of the best varieties for table use, the medium-sized potatoes having a sweet earthy flavour that is regrettably absent in others.

Our efforts to delay the maturity of calabrese broccoli have not been too successful – not that we are sorry to see the fine green heads appearing this month. With a large and varied supply of fresh vegetables available now it seems a pity to add one more, but I am pleased to say it was given an enthusiastic welcome in the kitchen. The early heading Green Comet is possibly the best that can be grown. The initial large dome should be cut in good time to allow the formation of plentiful side shoots, each to bear a smaller head which, in my opinion, are the tastiest.

After a slow start, the sweet corn has responded to warm soil, and the green sheathed cobs are now tasselling and need regular inspection to be cut in peak condition. Salad crops may still be sown, also beetroot and parsley; in the event of adverse weather in October they can be cloched. Cauliflower Islandia is producing good pure white curds but they must be protected from direct sunshine. That delicacy for some, the globe artichoke, carried on 2m (6ft) stems above attractice grey foliage, is at the right stage for cutting.

In the lower orchard, protected by tall hedging and surrounding trees, we pick our first plum. It is Rivers' Early Prolific, a spreading ugly-contoured tree that bears small purple fruit with a heavy bloom, deliciously flavoured for cooking or dessert. I highly recommend this variety.

The weeks seem endless between the last dessert apple of winter and the first of the new summer. The top orchard is devoted almost entirely to early and mid-season varieties and as we ride beneath their branches, cutting grass, the stages of development and ripening are eagerly observed. First to ripen is Beauty of Bath, quite small, heavily mottled fruit on a yellow base, sharply flavoured but sweet and very juicy. Often as early, and sometimes ready in July, is George Cave. This is an excellent little apple, crisp and moist, and in a good season the orange-flushed fruit are borne very freely. Both these varieties part easily from the stalk when fully ripe and need eating within two days for their flavour to be appreciated.

Fan-trained plums on the south-facing wall unfortunately took the brunt of the early storm and the crop is very thin. They are mainly Victoria, so famous in name and in flavour, the oval red fruit sweet and unbelievably juicy. In a normal year their fruit-laden branches arch over to the ground; for dessert, cooking and freezing purposes this plum is unequalled, and the surplus fruit are quickly sold.

Often escaping late frost is Oullin's Golden Gage, strictly speaking not a true gage but a golden gage plum. It is one of the last to flower and the ripe fruit is excellent for many culinary and preserving purposes. At least we have a reasonable crop of these to tide us over the winter.

After only two weeks' really hot weather, it is very noticeable that certain plants are infinitely more susceptible to such conditions than others. Even roses show a marked dividing line, some growing stronger, while others quietly fade. Is it in their breeding or does colour have a say? The deep red Alec's Red is always willing to bloom but Fragrant Cloud shows considerable die-back, the lovely Prima Ballerina's fragrant pink flowers go from strength to strength

Tulip trees, *Liriodendron tulipifera*, and shrub border on the upper main lawn

Dusty and precarious work. Stuart trims one of the old yew hedges, some measuring more than 3m across

but Troika hides its face. So far as I know roses have been grown
here for many years, and perhaps rose 'sickness' could be the cause.
Meanwhile, Mischief, Just Joey, Peer Gynt and Young Quinn
continue to flower freely.

A day's steady rain revitalises the whole garden; lawns green up,
dust is washed from the trees, tubs and urns take on a new freshness.
The growth of grass has at last slowed down giving us a welcome
break, but it is also the time when weeds can appear, and on a dull
day a selective weedkiller is applied to all areas. At the back of my
mind for several weeks, thoughts of hedge-cutting become a sudden
reality, and I rely on the keen eye of Stuart to give the hundreds of
metres of yew hedging their annual trim. It is a dusty, dirty task,
requiring strength and agility to tackle both the regular 2m (6ft) high
and 1.2m (4ft) wide avenue hedges as well as the 5m (15ft) monsters
with widths up to 4m (12ft). Given good weather it is a four-to-five
week job, and it allows the yew to make a protective 2.5cm (1in) of
new growth before winter.

The rest of us are also kept busy with green privet hedging around
the tennis court and the top orchard perimeter. Taking a little more
time and care are the formal box hedges on the terraces and in the
courtyard, the latter being the dwarf *Buxus sempervirens* Suffruticosa.
As so often is the case with all hedge cutting, the clearing up takes up
more time than the trimming. Several *Taxus baccata* Fastigiata, the
fastigiate yew, along the canal and bordering terrace steps, are also
clipped now to height and shape.

The rock and bog garden create a tranquil scene during August.
The lush green growth of gunneras, irises and rheums, almost
obscuring the running water of the bog garden, merges gently with
the wealth of colour up above on the rockery. Gunneras are 2m (6ft)
high, and the massive leaves can provide adequate shelter in a rain
storm. The rock garden is full of dwarf treasures as well as the
colourful blocks of helianthemums. However vigorous and sometimes rampant these rock roses can be, they are among the most
brilliantly coloured plants available. Alice Howarth, Jubilee and the
deep orange-pink Watergate Rose are outstanding, their only fault
being that they become misshapen and woody after several years,
when it is preferable to replace them. An admirable plant for trailing
over large stones is *Silene maritima plena*, its white, fully double
flowers carried on stems that radiate in all directions from a grey-
green tuft. Further campanulas flowering now include *Campanula*
Norman Grove, a light blue hybrid, the harebell-like *C. rotundifolia
olympica, C. E. K.* Toogood, which forms large mats of deep blue
stars, and *C.* Peter Nix, a strong and free-flowering hybrid

The immense and handsome *Gunnera manicata*, unsurpassed for growing by shallow running water

producing pale blue bells until October. Another beautiful variety with an equally beautiful name is *C.* Mist Maiden, its hair-like stems carrying countless little nodding white bells.

The dianthus family are well represented on the sunnier ledges. Waithman's Beauty, Little Jock and the taller Betty Norton are full of flower, and there is always interest in the yellow-flowered *Dianthus knappii.*

Forming large clumps of glossy leaves which have wonderful autumn tints, *Geranium dalmaticum* has glowing pink flowers that delight us all summer. Much less vigorous is *G. napuligerum (farreri)*, whose delicate pink cups with striking black anthers are in flower off and on for several months.

The sisyrinchiums are a diverse family ranging from easy, short-lived little alpines that seed freely over our garden, to some very choice and sometimes difficult plants of exquisite charm. One I possess is *Sisyrinchium odoratissimum* with slender rush-like leaves and straw-coloured trumpets, delicately veined. It grows to only 23cm (9in), is fragrant, and here seems reasonably well established in the shade of some hellebores.

Although sedums are more at home in the border front, there are a few species that make excellent rock garden subjects. *Sedum spathulifolium* Purpureum and the paler-leaved *S. s.* Cappa Blanca are attractive foliage plants, often ravaged here by birds, but *S.*

Campanula rotundifolia olympica

middendorfianum is trouble free, and the combination of yellow flowers above purple-red, narrow-leaved foliage is very pleasing. Both *S. kamtschaticum* and its variegated form are well worth including in the larger rockery along with *S. sieboldii* with its broad glaucous leaves edged pink and pale rose flowers spotted green. Introduced by that eminent plantsman Mr Joe Elliott at his Broadwell nursery, just a few kilometres from here, is the hybrid *S.* Vera Jameson. Its parents are brilliant foliage sedums, and the hybrid is equally spectacular with deep bronze purple leaves bearing flat heads of smoky pink flowers. It has deservedly gained the Award of Merit and a First Class Certificate. Other alpines of merit in flower now are *Teucrium ackermannii, Oxalis floribunda, Thymus* Doone Valley, *Penstemon hirsutus pygmaeus, Cyananthus integer, Potentilla atrosanguinea, Potentilla* Wickwar Trailer and *Dimorphotheca barberiae* Compacta.

A 1.2m (4ft) high stone wall retains the levels between my garden and the glasshouse section. Frost over a number of years has made the face shaly and produced scree-like conditions below. The exceptionally sharp drainage enables me to grow many choice plants here that perhaps would not be considered in the main garden. Several species of *Dianthus* including *D. freynii, D. microlepis, D.* Whitehills and *D. subacaulis* are finding the starvation diet much to their liking, as are *Edraianthus pumilio, Campanula arvatica* and *Viola hederacea.* This viola is irresistible, and although it is on the borderline of hardiness I will always continue to grow it. The kidney-shaped leaves are uniquely formed, and the white and violet flowers are held erect on 7.5cm (3in) stems. Light shade is needed with a cool root-run, and I only wish it would seed once in a while for me.

On the subject of violas, indispensable for the country garden, we grow one or two varieties of interest, including Irish Molly, coloured dusky bronze, umber and yellow, Prince Henry, with delightful purple and yellow pansy faces, my favourite apricot-coloured Chantreyland, and *V. labradorica*, with light blue flowers over purple leaves, for a cool shady spot.

I have high regard for the origanums, varying from the early golden-foliaged *Origanum vulgare* Aureum to the semi-herbaceous *O. laevigatum* carrying myriads of tiny crimson-purple flowers on wiry stems, an excellent late summer plant. The miniature hop heads of *O. hybridum*, borne on 25cm (10in) stems over grey-haired foliage, make this an attractive acquisition, and from Turkey *O. amanum*, with long tubed pink flowers, forms tight little bushes only 10cm (4in) high.

It is hard to single out herbaceous plants this month, as they all seem so colourful and worthwhile. Greys in particular play an important role, blending in and softening the general effect. Associated with grasses they are lovely. Over chalk, artemisias show off the varied forms of their silvery foliage to the best. Lambrook Silver is certainly handsome at 1m (3ft) high, but the very finely cut feathery leaves of *Artemisia nutans* make it, in my opinion, number one. I have it planted with *Linum narbonense*, where it accentuates the

Viola hederacea

gentian-blue flowers, and with dwarf campanulas. *A. n.* Silver Queen forms dense clumps of erect silver-white foliage, enough for cutting if necessary, and although it hates our wet winters it dependably reappears in the spring with renewed vigour. Not in keeping with the rest of the family is *A. lactiflora*, which is green-foliaged and rises to 1.5m (5ft), the creamy white flowers borne in plumes during this month. This is a good plant for shade – in the sun it insists on plenty of moisture.

Quite spectacular in a mixed border are the achilleas, the boldest of which is Gold Plate. Here it grows to 1.2m (4ft) and carries 15cm (6in) wide flat heads of yellow for many weeks. Slightly smaller is Moonshine, surely among the top ten herbaceous perennials; its grey-green foliage is attractive the year round and the clear light yellow heads retain their colour for a long period. Not quite so brazen but a personal choice is *Achillea taygetea*, whose mustard-yellow small heads and pastel-grey leaves will fit in anywhere.

Three asters under 60cm (2ft) in height, suitable for the front of a border where they can be individually admired, are *Aster spectabilis, A. thomsonii* Nana and *A.* Floras Delight. I just cannot fault *A. spectabilis*, whose slightly arching stems carry sprays of intense blue flowers with an orange centre at least until October. No support is necessary and it will cut well, so why is it that I never see this species in other gardens? *A. thomsonii* Nana is equally long-flowering with a shade more lavender in the blooms, and *A.* Floras Delight has deeply rayed lilac flowers fading to pink. Its growth is upright and less vigorous.

Polygonums are valuable in many situations and we have several varieties here including *Polygonum vaccinifolium*, covered with spikes of pink flowers as it creeps over walls. *P.* Arun Gem, of Himalayan origin, is entirely different in that the flowers are borne on tassels and dangle from branching stems. Beginning this month, I can expect it to flower until the frosts.

I must give credit to two geraniums just now, they are *Geranium renardii*, with large grey-white flowers that are veined purple over very distinctive wrinkled, deeply felted, grey leaves, and *G.* Russell Prichard, a prostrate carmine-red variety, with small sage leaves. Both need full sun and well drained soil.

In the borders, *Coreopsis verticillata* Grandiflora, *Echinops ritro, Heliopsis* Golden Plume, *Hemerocallis, Phlox* Prince of Orange, *Scabiosa* Clive Greaves and *Thalictrum dipterocarpum* are all outstanding.

Across the main lawn a shaded bed is devoted to the 'giants': *Buphthalmum speciosum*; *Cimifuga racemosa*, with its slender arching

(*Left*) The rose pink *Crinum powellii* in a warm corner. (*Right*) *Stachys byzantinus,
Anaphalis triplinervis* and *Carex variegata* Aurea, a trio that complement each other

spikes of ivory flowers; *Crambe cordifolia*; *Ligularias*; and, topping
them all *Inula magnifica*, with huge hairy leaves and arm-thick stems
up to 2.1m (7ft) bearing large, bright yellow, rayed daisies.

The Maids' Garden looks delightful this month, recent plantings
having taken a hold alongside the existing subjects. On the shaded
side *Kirengeshoma koreana*, after a slow start, shows us two or three of
its yellow flowers. By continued mulching with peat and leafmould I
am hoping to rear this beautiful plant; it already has moisture and
dappled shade, all that remains is to keep the soil acidic. Hostas are
much easier. I particularly like *Hosta fortunei* Aureo-marginata
grown with *Viburnum tinus*, and *H.* Thomas Hogg with its cream-
edged, broad green foliage. Anemones are very often slow to
establish themselves. We are trying *Anemone vitifolia* amongst shrubs,
and seed-raised *A.* × *lesseri* with hellebores.

On the sunny side there are further greys, *Anaphalis triplinervis,
Stachys byzantinus*, and the ground-hugging *Artemisia glacialis*,
providing an excellent foil for *Campanula* Peter Nix. The neat grey-
leaved *Centaurea hypoleuca* contrasts with soft pink cornflowers, *Phlox*
Chattahoochee and *Penstemon isophyllus*, a cherry-red variety from
Mexico making a 1.2m (4ft) high bush of upright stems. A charming
dwarf grass is *Carex variegata* Aurea, whose bright yellow and green
variegated leaves rise to only 20cm (8in) and contrast beautifully
with the copper-red foliage of the compact *Berberis* Bagatelle.
Bulbous subjects include *Ornithogalum arabicum*, one of the most
handsome of the star of Bethlehem family, producing umbels of
china-white flowers each with a darker boss. Not too successful here,

131

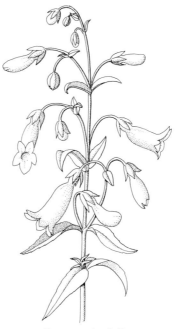

Penstemon isophyllus

it is nonetheless worth persevering with. Other bulbous plants are *Montbretia* Emily McKenzie with large orange-red flowers that have a striking sienna brown and yellow centre, and *Galtonia candicans*, with hyacinth-like racemes of milky white bells on 1m (3ft) stems.

Shrubs worthy of a mention must include the buddleias. On our limestone they make over 2m (7ft) of growth in height and spread and must be positioned accordingly. Cultivars of *Buddleia davidii* attract many butterflies on their flowering spikes, and in general this shrub creates a colourful picture as it rises above most others. The deep violet-blue Black Knight and the reddish-purple Royal Red are outstanding, but my favourite is *B. fallowiana* Alba which makes a more easily controlled bush of lovely silver-white foliage and bears countless white flowers, each with a golden eye. It needs a warm position as it is slightly tender. The other variety we grow is *B.* × *weyerana*, a hybrid between *B. davidii* and *B. globosa*, which has orange ball-shaped flowers borne on spikes on the young wood.

Potentillas are again prominent, the most noticeable being the white Abbotswood variety, a splendid 1.2m (4ft) high dense bush smothered with flower. The large-flowered yellow *Potentilla* Goldfinger is very bright amongst berberis, and for the border front or rockery the low-spreading grey-foliaged *P. fruticosa mandschurica* is seldom without its white blooms.

SEPTEMBER

This is an excellent month under glass. Odd days have a hint of autumn but generally speaking the weather continues to be warm and temperatures are more amenable to work in. Many plants quickly respond to the slight drop in day temperatures and the degree of humidity that comes with cooler nights, and some take on a new lease of life, with increased flowering and intensity of colour.

Stock plants of the regal pelargonium cut down in June have made strong fresh growth ideal for propagating material. Cuttings are trimmed to 7.5cm (3in) and the lower leaves are removed. The compost I use for all soft and medium wooded cuttings under glass is two parts sand and one part peat with a tablespoon of lime to the bushel. Apart from a fine spray to keep the leaves turgid, the cuttings require no other attention beyond shade from direct sun.

One little plant that really drinks up humidity is *Exacum affine*. I grow a large batch of them, as they are invaluable for greenhouse display and as a house plant during the autumn months. From seed sown in March they form tight rosettes of small shiny leaves and seem reluctant to grow much bigger until the end of July. They then thicken rapidly, especially if conditions are warm and moist, and by mid-September have nicely filled a 9cm (3½in) pot, which is ample for their needs. The flowers, which form quickly, are small, saucer-shaped and gentian-blue with orange stamens, a delightful combination, and scented too. A fine sandy peaty soil suits them well as long as nutrients are regularly applied.

Smithianthas often seem to be associated with much warmer conditions than ours, but I can assure you that they are a practical proposition for the cool house. Three years ago I raised a number of mixed colours from seed which, in turn, produced small rhizomes from which I grow fresh stock each year. Over bottom heat in spring they make a crown of brilliantly coloured leaves, dark green with purple, maroon and red zones and veining. By July they need a 12.5cm (5in) pot and low-strength feeding until the flower stems appear this month. The flowers are tubular, placed evenly around

The dovecote against a September sunrise

and up the 23cm (9in) stalks, and varying in colour from yellow to orange and apricot. Copious amounts of water are required in the height of the growing season, as well as shade.

Primula, cineraria and calceolaria seedlings in the frame are now potted individually and brought inside. A 9cm (3½in) pot will carry them through the winter until they are potted on in the spring. For a few days they are kept just moist to encourage them to root into fresh compost, consisting of, I would recommend, equal parts of loam and peat, and a half part of sand. The mixture must be fairly coarse and fibrous.

Quite distinct from other plants, the silky plumes of *Celosia argentea* Plumosa are always admired. This is a first-class pot plant by any standard. Easily raised from seed in March–April and needing a warm shelf in the early stages, their only fad is resentment of waterlogged soil, so that throughout their life the compost must be sharply drained. The strain I grow is Dwarf Fontana which makes compact plants a little over 30cm (1ft) high with scarlet, salmon, rose and gold plumes.

Cyperus alternifolius, the umbrella plant, must rank as one of the most useful foliage plants of all times. The insignificant flowers are of minor importance compared with its elegant growth and its numerous stems topped with a cluster of narrow leaves. It is a native of Australia and, because of its aquatic nature, demands huge quantities of moisture. Mature plants can be divided in spring, but by far the best method of producing shapely plants is to raise them from seed. This can be sown more or less at any time of the year provided that a temperature of 15°C (60°F) can be maintained, a condition necessary for successful germination. Seedlings appear like young grass, but soon take on the form of the unusual foliage. Once potted, lower temperatures are acceptable, and in the course of six months the plants will develop into large specimens. A 15cm (6in) pot can contain the strong root system and a liquid feed once a week is beneficial. Plants up to 1m (3ft) high are feasible as long as there is a constant supply of water; I stand mine in a saucer which is regularly topped up to supply these very conditions. Shade from strong sunshine and frequent overhead syringing will keep the leaves fresh and looking well.

Begonia sutherlandii is at its best now with masses of orange flowers tumbling over the staging, and the other species are also enjoying the cooler atmosphere. Late-struck cuttings of *Campanula isophylla* are flowering freely and will remain in small pots now. Streptocarpus are still a mass of bloom, Constant Nymph being joined by seed-raised forms in pink, mauve, blue and white shades. Impatiens, achimenes, torenia and coleus add to the colourful display, while fuchsias are bearing yet another crop of flowers after being shortened back last month.

Although we have nerines growing outside, their beauty can be considerably enhanced under glass. Their cycle of growth is in reverse compared with many other bulbous plants. Flowers appear this month followed by foliage that grows through until the early summer of next year, and it is during this foliage-growing season that the roots require ample water and nutrients. We grow two varieties, *Nerine bowdenii* Pink Triumph, with strong heads of crinkled pink flowers, and *N. undulata*, a narrow-leaved, more dwarf species, with rose-pink segments that are frilled along the edge. These plants flower most freely when in a pot-bound state and should only be re-potted every three years.

The climbing *Plumbago capensis* makes an attractive pot plant as long as it is kept to size by hard spring pruning. The phlox-like heads of ice-blue flowers are normally produced in September and October and are very pleasing. As long as it is well rested during winter, *Bougainvillea glabra* is a much easier plant to bring into flower than generally thought. Again, close pruning is essential to encourage the formation of new growth which will eventually bear the mauvy-pink bracts that surround tiny green flowers. Keeping the roots contained in a fairly small pot will greatly assist in flower production as long as liquid feed is applied in the growing season.

It only seems five minutes since we filled tubs and urns with zonal and ivy-leaved geraniums, and now it is time once again to take cuttings for next season's plants. Firm young shoots, preferably unflowered, are collected in the early morning and inserted into our cutting compost with a minimum of delay.

Plants that have stood outside for the summer months are brought under glass at the end of the month. These include *Azalea indica, Cymbidium* orchids, *Jasminum primulinum* and *Solanum capsicastrum*, along with the bulbous amaryllis, ismene and seed-raised freesias. Azaleas and solanums especially greatly appreciate daily syringing to help them adapt to dryer conditions.

The open-ground Charm and Autumn Queen chrysanthemums need to be potted fairly soon; some have made plants nearly a metre across and are a mass of bud. Early in the month the soil ball is cut on two sides, after which the plant is given a feed, and at the end of the month the remaining two sides are cut and the whole plant lifted and potted into a 20cm (8in) pot. They seem none the worse for this treatment, but alternatively they could be pot grown throughout the summer, although the resulting plants are never so large and compact. This does not apply to the large decorative chrysanthemums, which are grown in pots right through from the cutting stage and brought in as soon as buds are formed.

Seed sowing of greenhouse subjects is nearly over for this year, but a pinch each of trachelium, celsia, browallia and schizanthus will bring me additional colour in the late spring.

Tomatoes have been picked up to the third truss and now the question arises as to whether the lower foliage should be retained or removed. Schools of thought differ enormously. My own view is that while the leaves afford some protection for the fruit against direct sunlight in very hot weather, they should be retained, but when they have outlived their usefulness they must be removed. One of the main benefits of this is that air can circulate freely around the base of the plant, thus minimising fungal diseases. Another theory is that it hastens the ripening, as long as leaves are not removed above the ripening truss, and with this I agree. Always snap the leaves off with a sharp up and down movement, never do it in the heat of the day, and keep the plants well supplied with water.

The tomato plants have reached above the supporting wire, almost to the roof glass, and as there is little hope of further fruit trusses ripening they are stopped immediately after a leaf joint. Side shoots which develop very quickly are nipped out in good time, and

Sweet corn FI hybrid Early King

on no account must there be any check in the feeding programme. Often at this time of the season stems become hard and thinner, leaves have a slight yellowing and some of the lushness disappears. If this is the case, reduce the potash slightly once again and make up the balance with nitrogen.

There is an abundance of fruit and vegetables this month, and for once the kitchen is spoilt for choice. The first week sees sweet corn ripening in quantity, and a daily inspection of the cobs is necessary to cut them in perfect condition. When the tassels fade to a straw colour this is normally indicative of ripening, and to a certain degree this can be relied upon. But a more decisive method of testing for ripeness is to carefully ease back the tip of the sheath and feel the texture of the corn, which should be pliable and milky. This crop has the annoying habit of maturing quickly over a period of just a few days, and although the cobs are readily accepted the bulk of them, after careful preparation, are stored in the freezer. The mid-season variety Seneca Star follows by the middle of the month. This is a high quality corn, with slender cobs that ripen evenly and are attractive looking. Inevitably some cobs are only partially formed; the ripe kernels from these are shredded off and frozen, making yet another addition to the winter choice.

The small-fruited outdoor tomatoes look well after a warm August and are stopped at four trusses. I much prefer to grow them on a single stem and remove all side shoots, for although this requires a little more work the crop from each plant is greater. The ropes of fruit, looking like elongated bunches of grapes, are just starting to ripen now. The sweet distinctive taste and 'one bite' size make these tomatoes very popular for all salad dishes. Plants need a strong post for support and tying material of above average thickness, as the ultimate weight per plant can be considerable. To preserve moisture and prevent soil splashing we use a mulch of straw, and feeding is much on the lines of the glasshouse types.

We never seem to tire of fresh young runner beans, especially as their season, like many others, is rather a short one. Picking is every other day now, and any large 'seeders', sometimes hidden by foliage, must be disposed of as they can so quickly slow up continuous cropping. Irrigation should not be necessary this month unless in exceptional circumstances.

Pea-picking is slowing up, and now the rows are stripped and the best pods removed. Just how the late-sown rows will fare is anybody's guess, but if the weather continues favourable there could be a bonus crop.

Cabbage Stonehead has some fine firm heads, there are plenty of stump-rooted carrots, white turnips and beetroot, the maincrop calabrese broccoli Corvette will head up until the frosts, and cauliflower All the Year Round gives us the best curds of the summer. The old favourite lettuce Continuity stands well in the cooler days and takes on an extra sweetness; radishes too seem to possess a sharper flavour.

Marrows are swelling up and a big proportion of the crop is cut young as courgettes – this is the way I like them personally. A few will be left to develop into monsters but will, as so often, finish up at the harvest festival.

After a lull of three weeks we can once again start to pick raspberries. September, on our land the best autumn-fruiting variety, will now provide us with delicious wine-red berries, we would hope well into November. The opinion of some is that they lack flavour, but I strongly disagree: to me, their flavour is equal to that of many of the earlier types. A single strand of wire allows them to arch over just sufficiently to keep them clear of the ground. The air circulation is increased in this way, and also they are partially protected from heavy rain by overhanging foliage.

The last of the loganberries are picked, and there are a few perpetual strawberries as well as plenty of blackberries, both on our cultivated canes and in the hedgerows. Blackbirds are busy and squabblesome in the lilac walk, a sure sign that the mulberries are ripe. Our one black mulberry, *Morus nigra*, is an old tree with spreading branches and gnarled, almost cork-like bark, bearing good crops of fruit annually. The best berries are at the top, and the rather brittle nature of the young branches make it a difficult tree to climb, but a vigorous shaking of the lower arms will usually bring down sufficient for our needs. The fruit is only sweet when fully ripe and even then has a sharp acidic taste, but the seedy berries make a good filling for tarts and an excellent flavouring for ice cream.

Our other variety is the white mulberry, *Morus alba*, which stands as a specimen tree in the Maids' Garden. It has smooth, shining leaves and has just started to bear the long-stalked sweet berries, not a patch on the flavour of the black.

Side-growths on celeriac must continually be removed allowing as much sun as possible to the swelling roots. We start to blanch our celery about now; strips of black plastic are firmly wound around the stems and tied with raffia, and the soil is then drawn up. This process will continue over the next few weeks until only the leaf tops are left showing.

Towards the end of the month young spring cabbage plants are lined out, and there are also a few seeds to sow. Lettuce Winter Imperial is completely hardy and will form nice heads in late spring, with or without cloche protection, while a pinch of summer lettuce and radish will produce young plants in October and can benefit even further under cloches. Alternatively, sowings can be made in a frame, but generally speaking I find outdoor conditions with cloches will produce the best results.

There is no point in leaving maincrop potatoes in the ground after the end of September, as a more lengthy stay can so often result in slug damage. The two varieties we grow are Désirée and Majestic, both of which bear heavy crops and will store well for many months. Storing is quite simple: troughs of straw bales are made in a spare stable and the potatoes covered with loose straw, while in extreme weather a further covering of paper sacks will give complete protection against frost.

Ground that has produced peas and early potatoes this season comes into our plan for 'resting'. After rotovation and levelling it is sown with Italian ryegrass at the rate of 15g (½oz) to the square metre and will not be cultivated before late spring or possibly autumn according to land availability.

With the exception of bindweed we have eliminated most perennial weeds from the kitchen garden. Good cultivation can play an important part in weed control and in some cases the use of the hoe continually throughout the season will be sufficient to eradicate a particular weed. Annual weed is always with us; it comes in compost, farmyard manure and leafmould, as well as by airborne seeds during summer. Although easily controlled by hoeing there are a few varieties that, if allowed to seed, will increase dramatically. This month especially, cleavers, speedwell and mouse-ear chickweed seed profusely and at all costs must be prevented from doing so. The old saying 'one year's seed is seven years' weed' is absolutely true.

All raspberry canes that have fruited this summer are now cut to the ground and new ones tied in. Only strong straight canes are retained and I limit them to a 15cm (6in) spacing. On no account should they be shortened.

Seed of the quality maincrop onions for next year is sown during the latter half of the month. The two varieties used are Bedfordshire Champion and James Keeping. Ground should be thoroughly prepared and firmed, and a little superphosphate worked in. I always wait for a good rain before sowing, even if it means waiting until early October.

Further dessert apples reach maturity during the month, one I particularly look forward to being Ellison's Orange. Its skin is soft but firm, and when fully ripe this excellent apple has a musky scent. Worcester Pearmain tastes as good as it looks, crisp and very juicy, the flavour rather sweet and not unlike the alpine strawberry. Much sharper in flavour and equally juicy is James Grieve; the fruit is handsomely striped and the skin has a sheen that adds to its mouth-watering qualities. All these varieties must be picked in peak condition, and although none of them are keepers they will remain in good condition for about two weeks. One of the joys of apple growing is to be able to appreciate fully the individual flavours of perfectly ripened fruit.

The first cooking apple to ripen is probably one of the choicest varieties available, Golden Noble. The very evenly shaped fruit are a pale gold, sometimes with a slight pinky flush on the sunny side. A heavy cropper of disease-free fruit, it has no faults that I am aware of, and kitchen quality, I am told, is superb.

Our earliest pears come from the cordon-trained varieties on the east-facing wall. So often spoilt by birds or winds if allowed to ripen fully on the tree, they are best picked when green or as the colouring appears. We store ours on trays in the cool stone-built cloche house (which in fact was quite likely a pear store in days gone by) and use them as they become ripe. Two varieties treated in this way are

Fondante D'Automne, a medium-sized smooth-skinned pear that remains green until a slight yellowing indicates it is ripe, and Williams' Bon Chrétien. Perhaps the most widely grown pear, and deservedly so, the latter's bumpy yellow fruit are deliciously flavoured and juicy – a splendid variety in every way.

Apart from the Victoria plum we have several other types. They are mainly old misshapen trees, tall and productive only at the branch tips. Nevertheless, they are a valuable addition, especially if the Victorias are few and far between as this year. Unique in flavour because it is non-acid is Coe's Golden Drop. The large minutely spotted amber fruit have an apricot-like texture, and although they are sparsely produced in the best of seasons it is well worth the acrobatics needed to pick them.

To me, September is one of the most interesting and by far the most satisfying month of the whole year. The weather is so often settled and warm, grass-cutting is less frequent and hedge-cutting is nearly completed, so that now we are able to slow down just a little and appreciate the soft lines and mellowing colours of the plants that feature in our late summer display.

In full sun and where drainage is extra sharp, *Caryopteris* × *clandonensis* remains one of the finest dwarf shrubs for autumn; on limestone both the grey foliage and spiraea-like soft blue flowers are shown up to the best advantage, and it will flower for many weeks, well into October if the weather is good. Ours are associated with lavender and *Potentilla* Daydawn. To keep them bushy and well furnished with new growth, hard pruning is necessary in early April, as so often they appear lifeless at this time of the year only to show young leaves at the approach of warmer days. Two hybrids of great merit are Kew Blue, slightly darker than the type, and Ferndown, whose violet-blue flowers contrasts beautifully with a dark-leaved berberis.

Another shrub well suited to our conditions is *Rhus cotinus* Foliis Purpureis. An avenue of them leading out to the parkland makes a splendid sight; although they are quite old now, their twisting branches never fail to bear the coppery purple leaves and smoky plumes of fluffy flowers, and in the afternoon sun the colouring is breathtaking. They require little attention and can be kept tidy by removal of brittle dead tips as growth commences in April.

A sheltered sunny corner in the Maids' Garden has proved to be the ideal position for *Aralia elata* Variegata. This tree-like shrub carries heads of very attractive pinnate foliage sometimes measuring 1m (3ft) long; the creamy mahonia-like flower racemes are not

Cotoneaster horizontalis tumbles down some fine old steps

spectacular, but the white edging on young leaves make this unusual plant well worth growing. It is expensive to buy and often slow to establish, and if it is not sheltered winds can cause considerable damage – not the best of recommendations but you should not be put off easily, as it is worth trying to grow it. Patience is necessary, and the removal of any suckering all-green leaves will keep the colour variation true.

A refreshing break in form and colour are the various forms of *Eryngium*, or sea hollies, whose deeply cut foliage and thistle-like flowers in many shades of metallic blue make them excellent feature plants. The more dwarf forms include *E. alpinum*, prickly looking yet surprisingly soft to the touch with striking steely blue heads. The best form I have seen, but unfortunately never possessed, is *E. a.* Donard Seedling. Equally attractive and, I admit, a favourite of mine is *E. bourgatii*, whose spiny heads have a cold grey-blue effect set off by glaucous fingered foliage. *E. variifolium* is the least colourful of the family, but I include it on account of its white-veined foliage; *E. tripartitum* on the other hand is a much branched, 1.2m (4ft) high variety of great charm, the starry violet-blue flowers freely produced in a long succession. Rather shy in growth but possibly the best hybrid is *E.* × *oliverianum*, with stems and flowers of shiny metallic blue, whereas much more vigorous is *E. planum*, with small

142

violet-blue thistles in great profusion. By far the most striking variety is the biennial *E. giganteum*, often referred to as Miss Wilmott's Ghost. The green flower heads ripen to silver-white, the bracts are broad with spiny segments, and the overall effect is, as its English name suggests, ghostly. It is easily raised from seed, unlike the rest of the family who are often reluctant to germinate, but root cuttings provide the best method of increase.

This is not gentian country by any means, but a few species are tolerant of lime and provide delightful patches of colour. Apart from *Gentiana verna* Angulosa in the spring – and who can resist this gem of an alpine – we have the easier *G. septemfida*, generously clothing its stems with bright blue trumpets and thriving in almost any situation. For a moister soil which must, however, never be waterlogged, the willow gentian, *G. asclepiadea*, is a perfect subject. The arching stems carry the flowers in pairs from leaf axils, and the two varieties we grow are the pale blue Phyllis, and the much deeper Knightshayes. The New Zealand *G. saxosa* is quite distinct and untypical of the family; hummocks of bronze-green leaves carry numerous creamy white flowers on 2.5cm (1in) stems. In full sun and with plenty of moist grit at its roots, it unfortunately flowers itself to death in the second year with us, but I shall continue to purchase it or raise it from seed when available.

Metallic blue heads of *Eryngium tripartitum*

Quite by chance I acquired a plant of *Verbena* Sissinghurst, knowing full well that it would not be winter hardy here and that cuttings must be taken in late summer to winter over in a frame. Its vigour astonished me. One root produced a metre-square carpet of bright carmine flowers, and there seemed no end to the stoloniferous habit of this plant. I shall try it next season as a wall plant, and surely it must have great potential in tubs and urns.

Walls provide their fair share of colour this month, with clematis especially well represented. Rising to 3m (10ft) and then cascading down in a tangled arch is *Clematis tangutica*, the pale green foliage such an excellent foil for the myriads of yellow bells. Not only are the flowers the essence of a country garden, the seed heads that follow are like silver feathers and stay for many weeks. Pruning consists of shortening the trailing stems back to just above the thick woody branches during February, but in most cases I am content to let this rampant beauty ramble.

Ever since losing *C. armandii* in a hard winter I was at a loss to think of something with which to replace it. It was a good evergreen and the white flowers borne in April were always admired; at the same time it refused to be trained to any direction. I have now planted *C. flammula*, with the intention of tying it in up to a height of about 3m (9–10ft) and then allowing the dense branches to tumble down to show off the small white fragrant flowers during this month and October.

During the summer there are numerous varieties of large-flowered clematis making a huge splash of colour against the Cotswold stone. Among the best are Lady Betty Balfour, *C. × jackmanii*, Comtesse de Bouchard and the lovely white Duchess of Edinburgh. An outstanding variety that commences flowering now is Star of India; seldom seen or offered, it is a marvellous addition that can remain in flower well into November.

A few more campanulas are now in bloom: *Campanula* Molly Pinsent, with pale lavender bells over bronzy foliage; *C. pulla* with deep violet dangling bells on wiry stems just 5cm (2in) high; the lovely double pale blue *C. haylodgensis* Plena; and a recent introduction, *C.* Philip Boughton, a dwarf *glomerata* type with violet-purple flowers in clusters.

As a herbaceous subject for both decoration and cutting, the scabious has few, if any, equals. Revelling in well drained chalky soils, it bears its medium blue flowers on strong stems requiring no staking – no wonder that I rate it as an outstanding plant for late summer and autumn use. By far the best variety is Clive Greaves, reliable and long lived, while the best white form is Miss Willmott.

A seldom seen but interesting evergreen, *Itea ilicifolia*

An attractive carpeter is *Scabiosa pterocephala*, which, on a dry stony soil, bears its mauve-pink heads in profusion, while the smallest of all is *S. alpina* Nana, just 5cm (2in) high, with pale lavender flowers over tufts of indented leaves.

Lavenders have for many years been associated with the country garden. Some discretion must be used if they are planted in a mixed border, but as a dwarf hedge or edging they are extremely useful. As much as I like the old English lavender, *Lavandula spica*, it is a plant that must be given plenty of room; situated near the house its fine scent can fill the evening air. The compact *L.* Hidcote, or *L. nana atropurpurea* as it used to be called, makes an excellent dwarf hedge. Here it surrounds the lower rose beds in the pool garden and merges quite superbly with *Lilium regale*. The greener-leaved *L.* Munstead has dark lavender spikes and is better planted amongst shrubs or confined to a dry corner. Small enough to be included in the rock garden or border is *L. Vera* Nana Alba, whose white flowers on 15cm (6in) stems combine to great effect with the silver-grey foliage. A fairly hard shearing back when the flowers fade will keep most varieties neat and prevent them from straggling. Inevitably they became woody and less productive, but heel cuttings lined out in a shady position during July or August will make young stock the following spring. I have, on occasion, cut 2.5cm (1in) thick wood to

145

Schizostylis coccinae

the ground in April – a drastic measure not to be generally recommended – only to be rewarded with abundant new growth.

The bog garden remains lush and green. The candelabra primulas have finished flowering in any quantity, but *Primula florindae* has the occasional smaller stem of sulphur-yellow blooms. Away from the water's edge but in damp soil *Schizostylis coccinea* is flowering well and, with luck, will continue to do so for some weeks. The fans of iris leaves and 60cm (2ft) spikes of crimson flowers make this plant a valuable addition to the autumn garden. *S.* Viscountess Byng is a pink variety, slightly less tall, that has the urge to bloom all winter if weather conditions were ever that favourable.

Helianthemums again supply the bulk of colour to the rock garden, but as usual there are many less vigorous but more interesting plants to fill the ledges and slopes. A charming little plant whose roots will run in all directions in dry gritty soil is *Scutellaria scordifolia*. For most of the summer it remains as a carpet of small leaves, eventually producing a mass of upright stems, leaf-clothed, bearing deep indigo-blue hooded flowers at the top and from the axils. The same conditions suit *Frankenia thymifolia*, which, being of Spanish origin, naturally requires maximum sun to open the countless tiny pink stemless flowers over grey-green wiry foliage.

146

Hutchinsia alpina was never very long lived here until I planted it close to the water where it is shaded by a large stone from the afternoon sun. The small dark green leaves now form a 60cm (2ft) wide carpet that is sheeted with pure white flowers. Apart from the herbaceous varieties, the *Achillea* family contains some grey-leaved gems for the rockery. All are finely foliaged and need a collar of grit to protect them from winter wet; among the best are *A. umbellata* with white flowers and *A. argentea*, whose silver mounds look so well with dwarf narcissus in the spring.

The smaller-leaved sedums are worthy of inclusion in the larger rock garden as they contain varieties that are extremely colourful this month. An old favourite of mine is *S. middendorfianum*, whose bright yellow flowers are a perfect foil to the purple rosettes which turn bronzy crimson with age. Allowed to trail over a ledge, *S. cauticola* makes a picture, with rose-crimson heads emerging from thick glaucous purple foliage. A hybrid from this species is *S.* Ruby Glow; a first-class plant with a somewhat lax habit, its ruby-red corymbs rise on 15cm (6in) stems above grey-purple leaves. It fully deserves its Award of Merit and Award of Garden Merit. Perhaps the most colourful, and needing 900sq cm (1sq ft) per plant, is

Scutellaria scordifolia

147

S. floriferum Weihenstephaner Gold, with olive-green fleshy leaves covered with masses of starry yellow flowers.

An unusual potentilla for the rockery or paving is *Potentilla tonguei*. Displaying trailing stems tipped with orange flowers that have a maroon eye, it is a very worthwhile plant for soil that is not too dry. Other alpines of interest in flower now are *Hypericum coris, Polemonium pauciflorum, Silene schafta* Abbotswood variety, *Silene keiskii minor, Dryas octopetala* and *Anthyllis montana* Rubra.

Looking across to the herbaceous borders it is noticeable that while most subjects are still colourful and, in many cases, producing a second crop of flower, certain plants and colours dominate the scene. I remember some years ago when *Sedum spectabile* Autumn Joy was first introduced, it came from Germany with an unpronounceable name, and duly took on its appropriate present title. Its wide salmon-pink heads that slowly take on autumn tints, finishing as a dull claret red in October, put this sedum in the top ten of reliable, long-lived and attractive herbaceous plants. Seen at its best en masse, I plant it around sharp corners, under *Senecio greyi* and amongst foliage shrubs. Another of the *spectabile* group is Meteor; with its dwarf habit and cherry-red heads over succulent pale green leaves, it looks particularly fine with *Weigela florida* Foliis Purpureis.

The genus *Oenothera* includes several good perennials which are predominantly yellow, a colour often lacking in the autumn border. The prostrate *O. missouriensis* is an excellent wall plant as well as a gap-filler for the border front and rock garden. The pale lemon flowers are often as much as 10cm (4in) across, and although lasting no longer than two days they are continuously produced for three or four months. *O. fruticosa* Yellow River is the most free-flowering variety, with bright canary-yellow flowers borne on 30cm (1ft) high stems for several weeks, as long as moisture is not lacking at the roots. A recent purchase is *O. glaber*, which I had to acquire after seeing it at Joe Elliott's nursery. The leaves are quite distinct, oval shaped and the colour of burnished mahogany, while flower buds are formed in clusters and individually enclosed in a scarlet sheath before opening to a rich golden yellow, delicately veined. An 'evening primrose' of great charm, this is another plant that needs full sun but must not become dry at the root. Given these requirements, it will slowly form neat clumps.

Because I like fragrance in a garden I grow several forms of dianthus including pinks that have returned to cultivation after a period of undeserved neglect. By far the best scented is *Dianthus* Inchmery, with fully double pale pink flowers. I have admired and grown this wonderful variety for over twenty years, and taken it with me whenever I moved. The much more dwarf *D.* Charles Musgrave has single pure white blooms with an attractive green eye; its fragrance on a warm summer's evening is quite outstanding. Other varieties are the double red Emperor, the old pink and white Sam Barlow, and the rose pink Excelsior. All are happy in a well drained stony loam and need trimming back to basal buds in the spring to keep the clumps furnished with young shoots.

Again, various forms of asters provide us with solid drifts of colour, none so free flowering as *Aster acris* Nanus, whose clouds of small, deep blue daisies have an irresistible attraction to butterflies. *A. amellus* has given rise to several good hybrids of great merit – Violet Queen and Sonia are among the best – covering their bushy growth with a long succession of rayed flowers in shades of lavender blue and soft pink. I personally think that *A.* × *frikartii* is the finest variety ever raised. Associated with tall artemisias, the lavender-blue flowers look superb. I am not particularly attracted to the Michaelmas daisy, but by no means would I question its popularity – either you like them or you don't. I grow a number of varieties for the sole reason that they admirably fill a gap in the flowering calendar. Of the taller types, I have the large pale mauve Ada Ballard and the dark blue Mistress Quickly, both of which are strong enough to stand without staking. For windier positions and the border front the dwarf Lady in Blue and Little Pink Beauty are more suitable. In both cases they must not be cramped for room if they are

Fuchsia magellanica gracilis Versicolor

to be seen at their best, and yearly division, planting only the outer leafy clumps, will keep them strong and disease free.

Through trial and error several fuchsias have become permanent residents of the garden. Strictly speaking, they are shrubs, cut to the ground by severe frost only to make abundant fresh growth the following April. Only the toughest survive here – the red and purple Mrs Popple and the pink and violet Margaret are the only two proven varieties of complete hardiness. This is apart, of course, from *F. magellanica gracilis* Versicolor, an indispensable dwarf shrub used in a variety of situations, and especially lovely combined with ornamental grasses. The slender arching stems of variegated foliage carry narrow purple and red flowers from every leaf axil. It will also make a marvellous hedge in sheltered positions.

Speaking of grasses, I have long since appreciated their full potential as foils and focal specimens. The tall strong-growing varieties such as *Lasiogrostis splendens, Miscanthus sinensis* Variegatus and *Stipa gigantea* must be given ample room to develop and allowance must be made for the arching foliage and feathery flower spikes. At the other end of the scale we grow the Japanese *Hakonechloa macro* Albo-aurea, 20cm (8in) tufts of bronze-green variations, and *Carex variegata* Aurea, even shorter with green and yellow striped leaves. Both are non-invasive and choice enough to plant in the Maids' Garden. Our most recent addition is *Cortaderia* Gold Band, a New Zealand 'pampas grass'. With long gold and green narrow leaves, and silver plumes reaching 1.5m (5ft), it is worthy of inclusion on foliage effect alone.

Our ever-faithful family of potentillas have one or two more additions this month, the most interesting being *Potentilla* Vilmoriniana. With lax upright stems clothed with small silver-green leaves and carrying the creamy rose flowers at the tips, this is not the easiest variety to grow and is often difficult to please. Meanwhile the potentillas Daydawn, Sunset, Elizabeth and Beesiana continue to flower profusely and colourfully advertise the fact that they are among the finest of summer-blooming shrubs.

OCTOBER

During this month artificial heat will be necessary in order to continue the season as long as possible. The weather forecasts will often give some indication of approaching cold weather, in which case the heating system must be switched on, preferably two days in advance.

Night temperatures can fall quite dramatically in this part of the country, especially after fine cloudless days, and a daily check of the lowest mark on a maximum and minimum thermometer will often reveal surprisingly cool conditions. Equally important is the humidity level, and all damping down and overhead syringing must now cease in order to create a dry atmosphere, while ventilation must be carefully managed between 10 am and 3 pm to allow a gentle circulation of fresh air.

Plants are divided into two separate classes for watering: firstly those that require adequate supplies to keep them growing for the next two or three months, and secondly those that are approaching their dormant season and need gradually decreasing amounts to assist ripening of bulbs and rhizomes below ground, or woody stems above. There are no hard and fast rules for this process, just an understanding and regular observation of the plants in question. The second group consists of begonias and gloxinias, ismenes, arums, amaryllis and cannas. Feeding of these must now stop and moisture be reduced to a minimum over the next month as foliage starts to yellow. All dead leaves and flower stems must be removed to prevent any fungal infection, and all these plants will greatly benefit from as much sunshine as possible just at this time.

On the other hand we can still enjoy a display of colourful subjects for a few weeks longer. *Hoya carnosa* continues to produce its lovely wax-like flowers along the whole length of the now rather too vigorous stems, *Campanula isophylla* varieties and *C. fragilis* are still a mass of flower but need dead-heading regularly to keep them attractive, and *Exacum affine* provide small pots full of scented blue saucers. There seems no end to the streptocarpus season – both the

151

hybrids and Constant Nymph are full of flower and provide excellent material for indoor decoration. Coleus, browallias, smithianthas and celosias are also in good condition.

Whilst these plants continue to bloom feeding must not be neglected, but at the same time the intake of nutrients is considerably slowed down and liquid feed should be at half strength. The pot-tapper becomes a very important piece of equipment during the autumn months, for although to the eye the soil surface can look dry, the root ball may be just moist, and overwatering is a sure way of terminating a flowering season and, in some cases, the whole plant.

One of my favourite late flowering plants is the vinca, often listed as *Vinca rosea* or *Catharanthus roseus*. Whatever its correct name is, it remains a very useful and colourful pot plant. Raised from seed in April and eventually potted into 12.5cm (5in) pots, they stood in an open, slightly shaded frame for the summer with syringing and feeding weekly, and by September made bushy plants 30cm (1ft) high. Once brought inside they quickly come into flower, their colours varying from deep pink to white with a red eye, while the foliage is glossy and bay-like in appearance. One of the great virtues of this plant is that seldom is it infected with aphids or disease.

The scented-leaved pelargoniums embrace a number of species which can be brought into flower this month. By far the best method is to stand a few of each type outside for August and September,

Gardeners' cottages (Jacobean) in the village

having previously cut them down to firm wood, and introduce them to a little warmth, when new growth is freely made. Fairly dry soil suits them well, and you should keep them well syringed as they attract white fly from all around. Their leaves are fimbriated and crimped, and scent varies from citron to nutmeg. As a foliage plant *Pelargonium crispum* is wonderful, with gold and green variations that are seen to the full if the rather insignificant pink flowers are removed. If bottom heat is available, they can be propagated all the year round.

A few more cuttings of zonal and ivy-leaved geraniums are needed and these are taken from outside plants that continue to make a splash of colour in beds and tubs. Regal pelargoniums can also be struck as long as a 10°C (50°F) temperature can be maintained in a cutting frame.

By the end of this month I like to have all seedling plants potted up; rarely do they take kindly to movement beyond this time. Any others standing outside must be housed by the second or third week.

As many species look forward to their winter rest, the chrysanthemum is just beginning to reach the peak of its long flowering season. Although we grow several pots of the large-flowered type for halls and stairways, it is mainly the bushy Charm type that I rely on for decoration. After being lifted from the open ground last month, they seem none the worse for the upheaval, and whilst new root develops a daily overhead misting combined with a regular foliar feed will keep the plants in good condition. Their natural habit is one of dense multibranched stems clothed to the base with small bright green leaves; flower buds are produced freely and completely cover the tight domes. By the open ground method plants are kept compact with considerable spread, and no support is necessary at any stage. Flowers open slowly and evenly thumbnail size on the average, although some will reach 4cm (1½in) across. Colours vary from white to yellow, pale pink, orange and wine shades. Once they have settled into their 20cm (8in) or 25cm (10in) pots a high potash feed is beneficial. Liquid tomato fertiliser is perfect, the accent being on a little and often.

The other variety, treated in exactly the same way in all aspects, is *Chrysanthemum* FI Autumn Queen. The plants are a little taller than Charm but of equal girth, foliage is stronger and darker and flowers are fewer in quantity but individually larger. In the final stages the plants are of perfect shape, 45cm (1½ft) high and 60cm (2ft) across, and a crop of up to a hundred blooms is not unusual; the semi-double flowers come in a very wide range of colour including bronzy yellow and russet shades.

It is always a sad occasion when the tomato crop finishes. The season is relatively short but a highly productive one all the same: apart from the freshly picked fruit several kilos have been frozen and others puréed into pint-size cartons, providing excellent winter material for soups and sauces. Any unripe fruit are cut and placed on shelving to colour up. The green fruit of course can also be used for chutney. Plants are detached from the strings or canes and cut down to 23cm (9in) above ground level, after which they are taken out to be dried and burnt. The stump and root system are carefully lifted out, the reason for this being that an examination of the roots can indicate any faults in watering or fungal disease. If the fine roots are still pale coloured almost to their tips all is well, but any amount of dead brown strands mean a moisture disorder, an analysis of which can often lead to increased health and vigour of future crops.

The drop in our minimum winter temperature has also reduced the quantity of bulbs forced for early spring flowering. The word 'forced' is rather misleading; I prefer to grow them in an open cold frame, giving protection only from heavy rains, and introduce them to gentle warmth only in the final stages of growth. This way flowering is advanced by just three or four weeks, but growth is sturdy and healthy and blooms last much longer. The choice is endless: with hyacinths, narcissus, and single and double tulips the selected varieties are more often than not personal favourites, while generally speaking, pans of dwarf bulbs are appreciated even more and bring a real touch of spring to a cold March day. Most suitable, I find, are crocus species, *Scilla sibirica* Spring Beauty, snowdrops, *Iris reticulata* forms, and *Chionodoxa sardensis*. The half pot or seed pan is the best container for these small subjects, and the compost must be gritty and well drained. Nine bulbs to a 12.5cm (5in) pot will produce natural looking results, and a surface coating of stone chips will prevent surface algae.

In recent years considerable interest has reawakened in potato varieties, some of which are not commercially available but can be obtained from specialist growers in Scotland. One list I have seen numbers no less than 160 names. I have always regarded the potato as a highly individualistic plant, especially in the make-up of soils that suit the needs of the different varieties – depth, humus content and pH all play vital roles. The varieties we grow here have been tried and tested over a number of years; they suit this land, but grow them a short distance away and results could be very different.

I agreed earlier in the year with John and Stuart, both of whom have faith in some of the 'oldies', that I would put on trial varieties of their choosing and compare them with our regular types. Included were Kerr's Pink, Dr McIntosh, Golden Wonder, Pride of Bute, Ostara and Record. Out of these six, in my opinion, only Record had all the three qualities I look for: texture, taste and cooking adaptability. For roast and chipped potatoes it is the best I have ever come across, and although the remainder had at least one of these qualities, none of them possessed all three. Our two best varieties – and again I would emphasise, on this land – are Foremost for an early crop, and Désirée.

Japanese onions sown in August are now ready for moving to their winter quarters. Many people would disagree with me on this point; when these onions were first introduced to this country it was generally accepted that transplanting resulted in several losses during winter. I can confidently say this is not so, as all ours are transplanted from a seed bed and losses are no more than 2 per cent. A little extra care is taken in lifting to keep root damage to a minimum, and planting is on very firm land, preferably manured for a previous crop. No fertiliser is applied until late spring, and then it is a high nitrogen one.

The late sowing of peas has not proved very successful. It is a gamble that seldom pays off in this part of the country, and, as so often, the cooler nights have given rise to mildew. A few kilos of sound pods are picked, after which the row is uprooted and cleared.

Runner beans are another crop I am always sorry to see go. Pods are still being produced but lack the texture and succulence of earlier ones and are barely worth picking. The plants are cut down to ground level but the roots are left in; all this family carry nitrogen nodules below ground, which will be dug in during the next few weeks.

On the other hand, dwarf beans are paying handsome dividends. A small row cloched over at the end of September are bearing clusters of pale green pods that are surprisingly tender and tasty.

Some of our finest quality cauliflowers mature this month; not having to contend with hot sun, the curds are pure white and firm. Calabrese broccoli continues to be highly productive as long as the smaller side shoots are regularly picked. In both cases the surplus is frozen, but as both deepfreeze units are nearing their capacity some will have to be sold. For flavour, I think carrots are at their peak in October, when Chantenay Red Cored and a mid-season sowing of Amsterdam Forcing give us excellent roots. Inevitably there is damage from carrot fly and in some cases small slugs, but whilst the percentage loss is minimal I shall continue to ban chemical deterrents.

One pest that can do considerable damage to winter greens just now is the caterpillar. I have noticed a number of them on late cabbages and Brussels sprouts, more than birds can cope with, but a thorough drenching on a cloudy day with an organic insecticide will prove fatal to them. Apart from these and the odd aphid on broad beans we have had very little trouble from pests; the spring months were certainly not conducive to breeding, and regular hoeing to control annual weed often destroys the host plants.

Onion harvesting is now completed and after a few days of extra ripening time in the greenhouse the bulbs are stored away. Those for use during the next two months are roped in bunches and hung near a sunny window, the remainder are trimmed and placed in slatted trays. Hopefully, they will keep us supplied until next June.

Salad crops are still plentiful along with beetroot, turnips, cabbage and marrow. Some winter vegetables are ready for use, Brussels sprouts Peer Gynt and parsnips in particular, but I have always believed that both these crops are much improved in texture and in flavour by sharp frost, and whilst we have sufficient seasonal greens and root crops they will be left to improve.

Parsley seems extra lush this year; the spring sowings were headed back to prevent seeding last month and are now shooting abundantly from the base. Later sowings will stand through the winter and provide us with plenty of leaf until spoilt by extreme frost. Looking ahead to this time, half a dozen roots are carefully lifted now, potted, and placed in the cold frame until after Christmas when, with the extra warmth of a glasshouse, they soon produce ample fresh leaves.

As sweet corn, peas, runner beans and potatoes are cleared the vacant ground is cleaned of annual weed and any perennial roots dug out. It is never too early to think about winter digging once this is completed: all land that can be turned over before the end of December is an absolute bonus and provides us with the best areas for early spring cultivation. Compost must be brought in and allowed to dry for a few days before it is broken up and distributed. Our first heap is just over a year old and has rotted down to a black, friable cake, humus-rich and full of minerals and fine worms.

The alpine strawberries are almost finished and once again have proved how valuable they are in the kitchen garden, giving nearly four months of continuous fruiting. Who could ask for more? Our September raspberries also carry a generous amount of fruit and look like continuing to do so whilst weather conditions are favourable. A few Ghento strawberries complete the fruit salad.

Of the plums, The Warwickshire Drooper (what a wonderful

Returning organic material to the kitchen garden in October. An essential part of good husbandry

name for a plum!) is a yellow egg variety that ripens early this month and, although not tasting quite so delicious as it looks, is first class for preserving. The last to ripen here is Marjorie's Seedling, a huge black cooking plum that is also useful for dessert use if allowed to ripen fully. The tree is tall, and annual growth, even after forty years, is vigorous; the fruit has a metallic bloom and needs careful handling. This is another plum that sells on sight but is really rather disappointing in taste, although it is excellent stewed.

For flavour you just cannot beat a damson, so adaptable in the kitchen, a marvellous jam maker and a valuable addition for the freezer. It is something of a gamble as blossom is often nipped by frost, but in a good year I like nothing better than picking this delicious fruit. The variety is Merryweather, probably the most reliable as it is self-fertile. Planted with the protection of other trees, it is long lived and a good cropper.

Our most prolific pear, without doubt, is Conference. Even after a cold spring it unfailingly packs its branches with long green fruit which will ripen, if stored when they part easily from the tree. The majority of our trees are espalier trained and form an avenue either side of the central kitchen garden path. Conference's one fault is that it is not scab resistant and on our land cankers badly, but even so it must be classed as a top quality reliable pear.

Needing the protection of a wall is Durondeau, a long narrow pear flushed with coppery autumn tints and with equally attractive foliage. The flavour is good and it will ripen slowly, when stored, over a period of three to four weeks. My favourite October pear is Beurré Hardy, again russett coloured but much longer and heavier than Durondeau. Growth is strong and fruit is smooth and free of scab – a superb variety in every way.

If I had to select one dessert apple for this month it would have to be Charles Ross, which looks good and tastes good. The fruit is highly coloured and perfectly round, and when mature the skin takes on a sheen. This variety is seldom troubled with any disease, but like many other highly flavoured apples it needs to be picked and eaten within a few days. A Canadian variety that has become deservedly popular in recent years is Spartan. Its colour is quite outstanding, the darkest of crimsons, and the flesh is very juicy and crisp. The medium sized fruit are borne very freely and remain in good condition for several weeks. I find its flavour varies according to the summer: in a dry season it tastes musky and perfumed, in a wet one it is sweet and cidery. On numerous occasions I have seen this apple in the shops during winter, but by no stretch of the imagination can the flavour be compared with the fresh product.

Most of our cooking apples mature in November, but one that ripens now is Peasgood's Nonsuch. The enormous pale golden fruit are ribbed at the base and need picking as the skin softens, and the flesh is sweet and cooks to a froth. It does not keep and it often crops lightly – not the best of recommendations for a cooker – but the flavour is quite unique.

By way of compensation for the cold late spring the weather continues fine and mild; rimy frost silvers the lawns most mornings now but clears with the warmth of mid-morning sun. Conditions such as these are a very welcome bonus to the professional gardener; not only does it extend the growing season for possibly another month, but it also allows us to start the long process of tidying up in good time, which is reflected in the general appearance of the garden during the next few weeks. Quite wrongly, many gardeners look upon this month as the end of the autumn season, tools and cutting equipment are retired inside and enthusiasm is centred mainly under glass.

With us it is almost the opposite. A careful selection of late flowering shrubs keeps the garden alive, many alpine and herbaceous plants bear a light second crop of bloom, and mature trees everywhere take on autumn tints that no artist's brush could ever capture, especially effective when reflected in the still lakes or outlined against the ochre stubble of surrounding fields.

(Left) A good October pear, Beurré Hardy. *(Right)* Howgate Wonder, a fine November-maturing cooking apple individually weighing well over 500g

Viewed from the church the whole chine extending from the stone bridge over the bog garden up to the canal tunnel by the main lawn is a blaze of colour. Outstanding both in size and leaf colouring are the beeches, understandably so as they have the calcareous soil and moist root run that they so enjoy. *Fagus sylvatica* Riversii, or the Rivers purple beech, completely dominates the sloping banks of the water garden; the plum purple colouring is distinct and beautiful and accentuates to the full the gold stems of nearby weeping willows. I have recently planted young trees of the fern-leaf, *Fagus sylvatica* Asplenifolia (Heterophylla), and the purple-leaved form *F. s.* Rohanii. Both are slow growing and will replace some rather ancient *Malus*, eventually providing startling autumn colour in years to come. Other contrasting leaf and bark colourings are provided by *Populus tacamahaca*, the balsam poplar, *Corylus colurna*, the seldom planted but perfectly shaped Turkish hazel, and *Acer macrophyllum*. This Oregon maple is a magnificent tall tree for foliage effect: the large dark green leaves fade to a bright orange and the stems are a consistent mahogany-ruby colour for most of the year. It seems happy in our soil drawing sufficient moisture from the running water and will, we hope, be a tree of some architectural splendour when mature. Another tree I have introduced to this area of the garden is *Sorbus* Mitchellii, in my opinion the most striking of the whitebeams, with large round leaves that are dark green above the grey felted beneath. Although the cherries are predominantly known

159

for their spring blossom there are one or two varieties that have very attractive tints in their autumn foliage, the best of which is *Prunus sargentii*, whose crimson colouring is quite spectacular.

Moving up to the old shrubbery, a splash of colour behind lilacs and *Cornus* comes from *Parrotia persica*, a small wide tree of spreading habit with beech-like foliage that turns into a multi-coloured picture of crimson, pink, orange and golden tints. I know of no other tree that is so handsome at this time of the year and it should most certainly be more widely planted than is generally seen. It follows the habit of the witchhazel family, of which it is a member, in flowering in February. The small red flower tufts have crimson anthers but are freely produced only on mature trees. It will make a fine single specimen for the lawn and can be trained for a wall where it is not too important to have a fast-growing subject.

An unusual conifer of great botanical interest is the maidenhair tree or *Ginkgo biloba*. The fan-shaped fleshy leaves are soft olive green and turn a mustard yellow this month before falling. Careful placing will show this plant off to its best advantage, some protection from cold winds is essential and a degree of patience must be exercised before sizeable trees are produced.

Of all these foliage trees none, in my estimation, can match *Acer griseum*. This paper-barked *Acer* is well suited to this land but again needs careful planting to form well-shaped specimens. Both trees planted at the top of the church walk and at the lower end of the water garden are exposed to the cold north and east winds, conditions they do not like, and after forty years they are misshapen and sparsely branched. Two others were planted at the base of the old park steps and, protected by tall yews, limes and willows, these have grown into mature well-shaped specimens which are greatly admired all the year round. This month they are superb in colouring and bark effect: the trifoliate leaves turn to shades of orange and gold, pink and claret, quite indescribable, the trunk and primary branches flake and peel to expose the orange-brown bark beneath, and as the late afternoon sun filters through the tall limes the whole tree becomes alight.

Several shrubs are still very colourful, including fuchsias, *Hypericum* Hidcote and Rowallane, *Buddleia* × *weyeriana*, *Caryopteris* forms, *Choisya ternata* (the Mexican orange blossom) and a number of potentillas, the best of which are Sunset and Vilmoriniana. A very useful dwarf broom is *Cytisus austriacus*; the yellow heads appear from early September onwards and silvery leaves which are covered with fine hair add extra value to this attractive shrub. It is perfectly hardy and will retain its base branching habit if lightly pruned in spring.

Peeling bark of *Acer griseum*, a magnificent, eye-catching small tree for autumn colouring

Magnolia grandiflora Exmouth, a slightly frost prone but very worthwhile variety

Hypericum Rowallane

Either side of the south-facing entrance of the manor we have *Magnolia grandiflora* Exmouth variety. This evergreen is normally classed as a wall shrub, and what a superb subject it is, when sheltered from late frosts and cold winds. Rising here to 3.5m (12ft), though inevitably suffering annual damage from weight of snow it continually forms a dense round-headed shrub bearing the fragrant

Clematis tangutica

white waterlily flowers which open on a warm day to measure sometimes 23cm (9in) across. This is a plant that relies entirely on good weather conditions if flowering is to continue through this month, but so often the lower petal is browned by frost, in which case the flower does not open. I call it an evergreen, but in fact here it loses at least 60 per cent of its leaves to severe frost, only quickly to form a fresh crop of the shiny large leaves, which are a velvety copper red beneath in the early stages.

Clematis Star of India and Mary Bateman remain in flower on a warm wall, and although *C. tangutica* has rid itself of the yellow lanterns the silky seed heads are quite lovely in early morning sun. *C. flammula* is also colourful, and the small white flowers are surprisingly fragrant during this month.

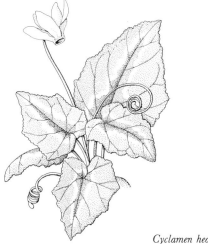

Cyclamen hederifolium

Hardy cyclamen can create unexpected patches of colour that give great pleasure to us all. Spring-flowering species have always been a failure due to mice and voles, our efforts to keep them at bay having been unsuccessful. Fortunately these creatures seem otherwise engaged in the autumn months, allowing us to grow one or two species of great value to the garden just now. By far the most reliable and hardy is *Cyclamen hederifolium*, whose natural habitat spreads throughout southern Europe and which is ideally suited to our climate. The rose-pink flowers with a deep carmine basal blotch often appear before the leaves and continue to unfurl their cylindrical buds until early November. As with all cyclamen, the foliage is extremely attractive, making a fine ground cover through to March. A close study of the individual silvery marbling will reveal that no two leaves are alike even from the same plant. Slightly smaller is *C. cilicium*; the pale pink flowers are more uniform in colour than those of *C. hederifolium*, and a very deep blotch at the base accentuates the delicate hanging blooms. The rounded leaves are slightly toothed and highly silvered, with reddish tints underneath. Both these species, and indeed most others, look well associated with dwarf shrubs, but given shade and a well drained leafy soil they will thrive for many years and increase liberally by seed. Although they cost considerably more it is well worth buying growing corms as against the dried up offerings which often take a lengthy time to settle in and flower.

Leucojum autumnale is a real gem for the autumn but needs careful placing if the small white bells on 12cm (5in) stems are to be seen at their best. Unlike some members of the family I find this species prefers full sun and sharply drained soil. A small group of them look wonderful at the base of a butcher's broom, *Ruscus aculeatus*, whose sharp pointed leaves of dark dusty green provide an excellent background.

A warm stony border against a wall provides just the conditions that nerines enjoy. The soil must be enriched with annual dressings of compost, and the neck of the bulb must remain just proud of the surface. The hardiest is probably *Nerine bowdenii*, its loose heads of pink flowers with curling petals freely borne during September and October and providing a startling effect when the bulbs are planted in quantity fairly closely. The other variety we grow is the hybrid *N. b.* Pink Triumph, just a few centimetres taller with a silvery sheen to the bright pink umbels. As flower stems appear, more moisture is needed to keep them sturdy, and during winter a mulch of bracken leaves or straw will protect the bulbs from severe frost.

Much hardier than is generally realised is the South African lily or agapanthus. Suitable for both the border and as focal specimens, this family of plants is extremely useful for late summer colour and they often remain in flower until the first frosts. Given full sun and not too dry a root run during the height of the growing season they make thick clumps of broad strap-like leaves over which the heads of flowers, sometimes numbering fifty or sixty individual florets, are carried. The recently introduced Headbourne hybrids contain shades of pale to violet blue and are among the hardiest. My own favourite is *Agapanthus campanulatus* Albus; with much narrower foliage and only 45cm (18in) tall, it has less dense umbels of flower, pure white and carried on slender stems that bow and nod in the wind. This variety is wrongly classed as tender, for in our garden it has survived temperatures of – 15°C (27° of frost) without damage. A large group are centred around a *Chamaecyparis* Stardust, a golden foliaged conifer of great merit and a perfect foil for the agapanthus. A new variety I have just planted is *A.* Bressingham Blue, bearing huge dark blue heads of robust form.

A first-class subject for the border front this month is *Scabiosa graminifolia*, with pale mauve flowers produced in endless succession on 23cm (9in) stems. The pink version, *S. g.* Pink Cushion is even better. Clumps of narrow silvery leaves give rise to charming pale pink, slightly rounded heads of flower that want to bloom indefinitely.

Equally at home on dry chalky soil is *Haplopappus coronopifolius*, another obliging and easy plant that remains in bloom from mid-summer to the end of October. Deep green serrated leaves form a wandering mat that carries deep yellow daisies in profusion on 15cm (6in) wiry stems – not spectacular, but quietly colourful when many other plants are fading.

During this month I make it a policy to carry a number of small envelopes with me to collect seed from many plants around the garden. In some cases this offers the best method of increase and there is always the chance of an outstanding hybrid cropping up, the

Haplopappus coronopifolius

dream of many a head gardener. The seed heads are placed in small plastic containers and allowed to dry thoroughly in the greenhouse before being packeted, dated and labelled.

Mild frost is frequent by the end of the month but a number of herbaceous subjects remain colourful. They include asters of all types, eryngiums, penstemons, fuchsias, rudbeckias and montbretias, to name a few. Grasses are also very handsome now, bearing their long feathery plumes of seed which make wonderful indoor decorations if cut in good time.

A real splash of colour comes from *Zauschneria californica* Dublin variety, a veritable treasure that regrettably does not survive our winter, try as I may. The sprawling twiggy bushes of silvery leaves are completely hidden by the countless stems of scarlet trumpets, greatly enjoyed by late insects. Cuttings are taken in September along with *Verbena* Sissinghurst and penstemons and are wintered over in a frame to provide us with new stock each year.

Violas also can be very unpredictable, flowers often appearing in the autumn and even up to Christmas in sheltered places. *Viola* Bowles Black and Jessie East are seldom out of flower at any time of the year, and although they tend to be annual they seed profusely everywhere. A quite unique colour of apricot orange belongs to *V.* Chantreyland, a great favourite of mine and reasonably long lived, easily raised from seed or soft cuttings in late summer. For light shade *V. labradorica* is an attractive little plant; the purple bronze foliage contrasts well with dwarf bulbs in the spring, and the scentless pale blue flowers appear from early April onwards. Two others we grow are *V. arenaria* Roseus, which is lavender pink, and *V. septentrionalis* Freckles, with white flowers heavily dotted blue.

Whilst these and other subjects continue to bear the last of their flowers we are content to leave them uncut and untidied, a tribute to their vigour and longevity of season, supporting my belief that October is the end of the summer and not the beginning of winter.

One task that I really like to complete this month is the pruning and tying in of all climbing roses. Having delighted us for most of the summer, they have ceased to flower now, so giving us the opportunity to tie in fresh strong growth to replace old wood that is cut out annually. On walls it is more a question of pruning to shape, as many of the very old species do not produce sufficient growth for replacement, and in some cases it is necessary to cut severely back a strong old cane in the hope it will burst into life from the base in the spring. Phosphates are often lacking on limestone, and a dressing of bonemeal this month will greatly assist in the build up of nutrients for next season.

NOVEMBER

During this month I have to rely on chrysanthemums to supply the bulk of decorative material for the manor house. Both the small-flowered Charm type and the large-flowered single and incurved hybrid forms are at their best now and make wonderful single specimens. Perhaps the best visually are the white and yellow 'spider' varieties, with graceful quilled petals that blend into almost any surroundings. Large multibranched plants can be produced from cuttings struck in February, and continual pinching out during the summer will develop a strong sturdy framework of stems that eventually carry a multitude of small flowers. For sheer effect I believe this is the best method, and the flowering season is extended over several weeks. If larger individual blooms are required then pinching out must be limited to twice, but as I am mainly concerned with indoor decoration size is not of primary importance. Blooms are not cut but presented as a growing plant, and as long as sensible watering and feeding are continued they remain colourful over a long period.

It is often at this time of the year that the variety of plants is limited under glass, but with some imagination and ingenuity a number of subjects usually associated with outdoor conditions can be seen as attractive pot plants. The most rewarding of all is the fibrous-rooted *semperflorens* begonia, grown from a late spring sowing specifically for this purpose or from mature outdoor plants carefully lifted and potted during October. Of the two methods the former will produce the best results but entails much more work, as the young plants in pots placed in a lightly shaded frame for the summer need constant watering and feeding as well as de-blossoming up to September. If only a few plants are required then the latter method is more economical and often produces equally good results. After lifting the plants are kept in a shaded frame for a few days and syringed overhead to encourage new growth. When young shoots at the base are evident the top stems and flower heads are carefully trimmed back and the plants brought into the plant house where, in

167

a temperature that averages 10°C (50°F), they soon break into bloom again. With careful watering and low-strength feeding, these cheerful little begonias delight us for many weeks to come.

When the moon is waxing, night frost is inevitably followed by sunshine and it is on these days that every opportunity should be taken to admit fresh air by careful ventilation, normally for two hours either side of midday. Not only does it clear glass of condensation but also goes a long way in preventing mildew and other fungal diseases so easily promoted in damp airless conditions. From the plants' point of view I am quite sure a gentle stream of fresh air is a real tonic, and on the warmest of days the side ventilators should be opened just sufficiently to encourage the maximum circulation.

Rarely seen as a pot plant, the salvia is wellnigh indispensable for early winter flowering, and the various scarlet forms of *Salvia splendens* coupled with the blue *S. patens* make useful additions to the cool house. Although both varieties can be propagated from cuttings, the best and most shapely plants are raised from seed sown during April. A bottom heat of 15°C (60°F) is necessary for even germination, and the young plants are potted into 7.5cm (3in) clays as soon as two pairs of leaves are formed. In June they are transferred to an open frame and potted on into 14cm (5½in) or 16cm (6¼in) pots according to resulting growth. Liquid manure must be given weekly and an overhead syringing is greatly appreciated by all this family, growing points should be pinched out regularly to keep a bushy habit and premature flowers removed up to mid-September. It is important to house them whilst the weather is warm, and under suitable conditions they will commence to flower during October and on into December, brightening the dull days with their brilliant colouring. *S. patens* is my favourite; its intense gentian-blue hoods are superb and make it one of the finest blue-flowered plants that can be grown. A word of warning; white fly find them irresistible and must be rigidly controlled.

Cherry pie or heliotrope is another subject that can be brought into flower this month – in fact, by regulating the production of young plants from cuttings or seed there are few months when this plant is not in flower. I grow it mainly for its fragrance and its colour, which varies from lavender to dark blue according to the variety. One of the best is Lord Roberts, which can only be propagated from cuttings, with beautiful dark foliage and violet flowers, but modern seed strains will also produce very satisfactory results. The compost should be an open one with the addition of leafmould, and several stoppings are necessary to form bushy specimens. This is a plant that will make excellent standards up to 90cm (3ft) high, but for volume of flower the bush form is more desirable.

Looking around I see that a few summer-flowering plants are still colourful and seem unwilling to call it a day. They include coleus, rather sparsely leaved now but suitable for fillers in large displays, *Exacum affine*, which I am quite sure would flower for months on end if more heat was available, *Browallia speciosa major, Beloperone guttata, Hoya carnosa* and my ever-faithful *Trachelium coeruleum*.

Cuttings of zonal, ivy-leaved and regal pelargoniums taken in September have rooted well and now need potting individually. Compost is a loam-based one with the addition of extra fine grit to eliminate the possibility of waterlogging in the 9cm (3½ in) pots during winter. Regal pelargoniums are placed in the warmest position possible as they are more tender and will not make new root under damp cool conditions.

By the end of the month foliage of most of the bulbous plants has dried off and can now be removed. They require no attention during the winter and can be stored away on staging or underneath as long as they remain perfectly dry. Standard fuchsias are almost dormant but a very small quantity of water applied once a fortnight will keep the woody system from drying out completely, thus assisting the new growth to form when pruning is carried out next February.

Foliage plants are not so affected by this month's lower temperatures and provide valuable display material. Both *Asparagus sprengeri* and *A. plumosus nanus* are attractive the year round, and another useful subject is *Chlorophytum comosum (elatum)* Variegatum, the easily grown spider plant. This bears cascades of leafy rosettes that colour better in light shade, and is an excellent plant for wall containers. *Plectranthus* will grow happily for a week or two yet, the fleshy *P. australis* often taking on rusty tints if feeding is stopped, while the variegated *P. coleoides* Marginatus looks extremely handsome among large dark-leaved plants such as *Aralia sieboldii (Fatsia japonica)* or *Cissus antarctica*, the kangaroo vine. I can never enthuse over ivies but two forms which I find particularly useful are *Hedera helix* Goldheart, with olive-green and yellow variations, and *H. h.* Tres Coupe, a close-growing trailer with pointed leaf ends.

Tradescantias in all their forms and colourings are indispensable. Cuttings taken now will make extra good plants by early spring, and over a little warmth they quickly root. Possibly the best way to display them at their best is by placing three plants in a 12.5cm (5in) half pot, for they seem to enjoy a shallow root run as long as the compost is fairly rich and feeding is not neglected.

It is not possible to generalise over weather conditions in the months prior to Christmas – indeed, the pattern can change dramatically in distances of less than 80km (50 miles). In the Cotswolds, during the last five years, there has been a very marked tendency for these months to be fairly mild and dry with light to medium frosts, followed by late, cold wet springs that cause many problems to the professional gardener. This year is no exception, and for most of November we continue to enjoy some very friendly weather allowing us, on numerous days, to work in shirt sleeves. Frosts are crisping the ground and creating perfect conditions for winter digging: the top spit cuts and lifts with little breakage off the spade, exposing the maximum area to the elements. It is of utmost importance that the land is composted and dug as it becomes available after clearance of summer crops, and at least a quarter of our day, every day, is taken up doing just this.

I am always sorry to see salad crops finish for another year; although we shall continue to cut lettuce during this month from under cloches the quality is never the same in comparison with the quick-growing summer varieties. Onion White Lisbon will stand in good condition for several more weeks and beetroot Boltardy is still firm and tender, so all is not lost.

We are fortunate that we have a few remaining cauliflowers. Islandia has proved to be the best for late heading, and although frost will almost certainly spoil them, cloche protection can extend their season until the end of the month. Not that we are trying to protect crops from frost – just the contrary, as we welcome it to improve the flavour and texture of winter brassicas and root crops. Brussels sprouts, in particular, are vastly improved by such conditions and our early crop of Peer Gynt are just beginning to mature. We grow a large quantity of this very dependable variety, and it is essential, as picking commences, to take a few buttons, from the base upwards, from as many plants as possible to ensure a continuation of firm sprouts up the whole length of stem. Some lower leaves will always yellow this month and these are best removed, with no detriment to the plant, allowing a free circulation of air and maximum exposure to frost. The true qualities of Peer Gynt are its ability to produce top-quality sprouts to the very top over a long period, and the sturdy habit that keeps the plant upright against weight or weather.

Of unique flavour, the parsnip is always in great demand here. Freshly dug and cooked it is a delicious vegetable, yet surprisingly it is not over-popular – you either adore them or you don't. Being completely hardy and actually improving in quality as frost becomes severe, parsnips can be lifted in all but ground-hard conditions throughout the winter. On this land there is always the tendency to canker, but by trial and error I have found Avonresister the least susceptible.

Autumn King carrot has produced a fine crop of cylindrical stump-ended roots. By far the most suitable variety on our shallow land, they are lifted as required. I am not too enthusiastic about storing carrots, as flavour quickly deteriorates; however, a little extra soil earthed over the crowns will afford some protection, and I much prefer this method whilst weather conditions are reasonable. Swedes, on the other hand, do not winter well here and are best used before the end of the month. They are not asked for in any quantity but remain a very useful addition in the kitchen.

Celeriac reaches prime condition this month and over the last few years we have grown increasing quantities to meet the growing demand. I have at last convinced the kitchen staff what a tasty and diversely used vegetable it is. Again they are lifted as needed – there is no substitute for the fresh product – but the bulbous roots are only able to withstand a limited degree of frost after which they can be seriously affected. Fortunately, this is one vegetable that will store very well for about two months, so as frosts become sharper at the end of this month the remaining roots are lifted, cleaned of root and tops, and placed in deep boxes of dry sand in a cool but frost-free situation.

The early batch of leek Autumn Mammoth have made some first class stems and are ready for lifting, but whilst we have a good variety of other vegetables for the kitchen I shall let them stand for a while. They are perhaps the hardiest of all winter crops and a great standby when the weather is severe, as they are completely unaffected by temperatures of $-10°C$ or less (twenty or more degrees of frost). We make it a policy not to apply any fertiliser to leeks, a thorough preparation of the ground initially with heavy dressings of organic material being all that is necessary to produce excellent table-quality stems.

By far the best cabbage this month is Minicole, a ball-headed variety of Dutch origin that is only medium sized but very hard and tight, it will stand in good condition for several weeks and is a first class variety for coleslaw. Red cabbage is also ready and is best picked before the worst of the winter weather arrives. It has a limited use as a fresh vegetable but is extremely useful for pickling.

There is still plenty of perpetual spinach beet, fresh parsley under open-ended cloches, chives and scallions. The last picking of herb leaves is made for drying in the boiler house.

171

Some of the best pears are picked during this month; in most cases they are not fully ripe but stand a better chance of maturing if trayed out under cover. Our most reliable cooking variety is Pitmaston Duchess, whose hardiness and high fertility result in heavy crops most years. The greeny yellow fruit carry a brown russet and do not taste quite as good as they look, but cooked or bottled they are excellent. Our cordons are loaded but the heaviest and most remarkable crop comes from a single old seven-tiered espalier that unfailingly bears over a hundred fruit.

Although not such a strong grower, Joséphine de Malines is probably the best winter dessert pear, and when carefully stored the fruit become melting and sweet flavoured. On a warm wall the abundant spring flower will set well. Two other varieties we grow, which are seldom listed nowadays, are Flemish Beauty and General Toddler, both storing successfully and ripening during December. Last but not least is Doyenné du Comice, a delicious juicy pear that should be included in every garden. Many people fail with this variety because it is a shy pollinator. Planted with Beurré Hardy there are no problems, but it really does appreciate a little extra attention to manuring and watering.

Generally described as the best dessert apple in the world, Cox's Orange Pippin is just this in my opinion. Needless to say, this is an apple for warm, wind-protected sites and needs a regular feeding programme if quality is of the first importance. Maturing throughout November the juice-laden fruit must be picked when fully ripe for its superb flavour to be appreciated to the full. It will also store reasonably well: individual wrapping can go a long way in keeping the skin moist, but the unique flavour of the fresh apple inevitably fades.

I find Blenheim Orange is almost as good, perhaps lacking the sharpness of a Cox but nevertheless a fine apple. The crimson streaked fruit are large and must be harvested just before maturity to prevent the skin drying. It originated just 20km (12 miles) away from here and makes a well shaped disease-free tree. Golden Delicious has received much criticism in the last decade, mainly because this country is flooded with foreign imports of inferior quality that bear no resemblance to the fresh product. The pale yellow fruit are flecked and spotted with rusty cinnamon, the flesh is firm, crisp and juicy and again must be sampled perfectly fresh.

Our last dessert apple for this month is Idared; the greenish yellow fruit are flushed crimson and the flavour is mild, but because it is not over-juicy it possesses excellent keeping qualities and is one of the few we store for new year use.

The list of cooking apples seems to begin and end with one name, Bramley Seedling. Its keeping quality is quite remarkable, its flavour is outstanding and the flesh is rich in vitamin C – what more could anyone want? This is not a variety for the small garden, as trees are vigorous and wide spreading and the weight of fruit in a good season is bough-bending. Our avenue of young trees in the kitchen garden provide us with quality fruit for storing, the huge old trees in the bottom orchard bear good apples mainly at the top and present difficulties for picking.

I must mention just one more cooker, Newton Wonder. Its habit of biennial bearing makes it not over popular, but it can be forgiven when it produces a crop of the golden fruit, striped and flushed red. It is one of the most disease-free apples I know, the flesh is white and juicy and of fine flavour, and its greasy skin will keep it in good condition, when stored, until February or March.

Quite suddenly, usually after sharp frost, the garden changes dramatically; colour fades from the herbaceous borders, lawns have an autumn greyness and the fiery tints of trees vanish for another year as leaves begin to fall. There are individual plants that will brighten the odd corner for a few days yet – some seem very unwilling to bow their heads to the weather and remain colourful, especially when protected from cold winds. The rudbeckias, Deamii in particular, continue to carry their dark-centred deep yellow flowers and scabious Clive Greaves is equally persistent. *Linum narbonense, Aster* Violet Queen and *A. thomsonii* Nana show us the last of the 'blues' and, along with violas, fuchsias, sedums and achilleas, provide late patches of interest.

All too often a garden can die with the approaching dormancy of deciduous trees and shrubs, while borders become empty as herbaceous plants retire below ground and the rock garden dwindles away. It is now that the backbone of the garden – its evergreen subjects – becomes prominent. With their wealth of leaf colouring, attractive flowers and long lasting berries, the evergreens carry the diversely planted garden through to the early spring. Well represented here is the genus *Cotoneaster*, containing prostrate, semi-upright and pendulous forms presented as a bush or small tree, and several kinds make excellent wall or bank coverers. Without doubt my favourite is *C. franchetii*, strictly speaking a semi-evergreen but never without the small dark green leaves which have a silvery reverse. Its slender stems arch gracefully under the weight of orange-scarlet berries that are freely borne, and altogether it is a shrub of great merit, equally happy in full sun or light shade and

Rudbeckia Deamii

goodnatured enough to respond to pruning to shape when necessary. The large bunches of creamy yellow berries make *C.* Exburiensis quite distinct, and its multi-directional growth will form a wide spreading bush or small tree of pale green foliage, again slightly silvered on the reverse. *C. henryanus* is a splendid variety; at home on a wall or as a loosely clipped background hedge, its willowy stems bear long olive-green heavily veined leaves that take on autumn tints, and the clusters of red berries are large and shiny.

Although *C. lacteus* is frequently nipped by sharp frost and resents cold winds, it is certainly well worth growing. The densely formed growth and dark leaves look extremely well in a sheltered corner and the small clusters of currant-sized berries do not fully colour and ripen until the depths of winter. The most spectacular variety here is *C.* × *watereri*, a hybrid between *henryanus* and *frigidus* which has developed into a medium-sized tree. The habit is open but rather stiff, defoliation can follow severe cold, but the grape-like bunches of scarlet berries in great profusion are a lovely sight during this month.

Several dwarf forms are very useful in the large rock garden. *C. microphyllus* disguises one of our waterfall outlets and permanently provides rigid weeping congested branches of very dark leaves that

174

carry carmine pink round berries in early October. Needing ample room and widely used as a ground coverer is *C. dammeri*, which forms thick mats of long prostrate shoots covered densely with oval leaves and studded with cherry-red berries during the autumn. *C. congestus* Nanus is a miniature gem where space is at a premium; twiggy mounds of slow-creeping stems are covered with very small shiny round leaves, and it likes nothing better than to follow the contours of a moist rock.

Last but not least, we have *C. horizontalis*; the arching herring-bone branches are well suited to walls and banks, but in my estimation it is seen at its best cascading down steps or retaining walls. It is not evergreen – foliage departs with autumn conditions – but the plentiful red berries remain attractive and colourful until Christmas.

One of the most versatile evergreens is *Aucuba japonica*, withstanding rough treatment and even dense shade, though it gets neither here. Our spotted female form is *A. j.* Variegata, planted in a south-facing position with the deciduous pink *Ceanothus* Marie Simon and displaying speckled golden yellow leaves, everlastingly bright. Some forms are better than others and the trees should be seen before being purchased. Regrettably, ours suffers snow damage annually and has to be pruned to shape each spring, yet after such treatment

Large pinnate leaves and fragrant flowers of *Mahonia japonica*, which provides colour most of the winter

the new clusters of fresh leaves are even more highly coloured, probably enhanced by our limy soil. One condition it insists on is ample supplies of water in the dryest summer months.

The firethorns, or *Pyracantha*, can barely be rivalled for adaptability and display of berries in many colours which have evolved with the introduction of improved cultivars in recent years. One of the most vigorous is *P. gibbsii (atalantioides)* with large dark leaves and plump crimson-scarlet berries. The newer *P.* Orange Charmer has even larger clusters of orange fruits, but for sheer quantity of small orange-scarlet berries *P.* Orange Glow is way ahead. I must also mention a much older cultivar of great hardiness and strong upright growth, *P. coccinea* Lalandei – the two we have in the small courtyard are never-failingly covered with bright orange-red fruit in the depths of winter. I have recently seen the variegated *P. c.* Harlequin, and the combination of coppery stems with cream-margined leaves is indeed very striking, but as yet I am not sure of its fruiting capabilities.

A word of praise for the *Euonymus*: the dwarf-growing evergreen forms are excellent subjects for the mixed shrub border and will tolerate without fuss comparatively deep shade. Two varieties I grow and like in particular are *E. fortunei* Emerald and Gold, with gold, green and sometimes pink-tinged leaves, quite outstanding for foliage effect, and the spreading *E. f.* Silver Queen, the cream and silvery stripes being extra bright in early spring.

I should dearly love to be able to grow *Elaeagnus pungens* Maculata – the irregular gold splashes on each leaf brighten the greyest of winter days – but it just will not settle down here. Perhaps it dislikes our chalky brash, but we shall persevere and hope.

The skimmia is often shunned because of its laurel-like leaves, but personally I class it as an invaluable evergreen that associates so well with narcissus Tête à Tête or W. P. Milner, and in light shade is a marvellous foil for yellow primroses. It is not a lime-lover by any means but regular dressings of Epsom salts will prevent fading of leaf colour. The variety we grow is the male form of *S. japonica*, which is covered with cones of fragrant starry white flowers during March and April.

Viburnums once again play an important role this month. The autumn-tinted leaves of *Viburnum opulus* Compactum have long since gone, but the loose clusters of glossy scarlet berries will remain with us for a few weeks more. The giant *V. rhytidophyllum*, always attractive, goes through a colour change in its fruit: the wide heads of red berries now turn black and viewed from below contrast sharply with the tomentose leaf reverse. Already *V. tinus* and its

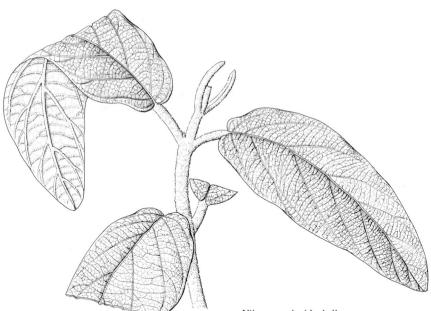

Viburnum rhytidophyllum

variegated form are budding up, and *V. fragrans* can be expected to flower from now on through the winter.

Other leaf colourings worthy of note come from *Rosa rubrifolia* and F. J. Grootendorst, *Catalpa bignonioides*, *Hydrangea petiolaris*, *Parrotia persica*, *Acer macrophyllum* and *Sorbus hupehensis*. Due to the relatively mild autumn the old gold leaves of *Liriodendron tulipifera* remain quietly beautiful in winter sunshine, and *Sorbus intermedia*, the Swedish whitebeam, bears red fruit on its leafless branches.

Several seed heads are worth collecting for decoration and these include *Echinops ritro*, *Eryngium planum*, *Centaurea pulchra major*, *Limonium latifolium* and the ornamental grass *Miscanthus* Silver Feather.

These are just a few of the berried and leaf-colouring subjects that keep the late autumn garden alive, emphasising the importance of maintaining a balance between deciduous and evergreen plants and trees. Evergreens in particular, at this time of the year, play a dual role providing screening as well as shelter from the wind, while leafless branches of deciduous trees are often superbly outlined against pale grey skies. Even the bark of *Cornus*, willow, *Robinia* and *Acer* can add colour and interest to the well planned garden.

DECEMBER

Under glass this is the least colourful and productive month of the year, regretably so for, with the approach of Christmas, as much flowering material as possible is needed for indoor decoration. Our lower temperature range has greatly reduced the list of varieties that will flower during this month. Gone are the days when a wealth of colour from cyclamen, primulas, *Euphorbia pulcherrima* (poinsettia) and hyacinths was available, and now we depend on a few old favourites with the addition of greenery. Fortunately we have held back the last of the hybrid pot chrysanthemums, and these will make excellent large focal specimens for the hall and stairways, especially if a few *Asparagus plumosus nanus* and *A. sprengeri* can be fitted in around the base.

The ever popular winter cherry, *Solanum capsicastrum*, although not a spectacular plant, is indeed a very valuable one and the cheerful red berries against dark foliage provide a very welcome subject in form and colour. It is now available in several attractive colour breaks, berries can be white, orange or red and growth can vary from the compact little Jubilee to the vigorous open habit of Red Giant. All need a fairly humid atmosphere to extend their season well into February or March, the compost must be open and fibrous, and weak liquid feed must be applied weekly to keep the foliage in good condition. It is generally accepted that they will spend their entire life in pots, having been raised from seed in early spring. However, to produce extra large specimens I revert to the old fashioned method of growing open ground plants which are fed and syringed throughout the summer, and carefully lifted in September to make large bushy plants, well balanced in fruit and foliage, for Christmas.

The odd *Primula malacoides* is in bud and *Begonia fuchsioides* has a fresh crop of deep pink flowers, always acceptable; along with a few primroses and potfuls of viola Jessie East, lifted from my garden, these help to swell the ranks. Foliage plants available include *Grevillea robusta*, chlorophytum, tradescantia, plectranthus and asparagus, while berried holly is cut from the woodlands and sprays of cotoneaster, *Prunus* and viburnum from the garden, all amounting to an adequate supply of material to decorate both manor house and church.

We must not forget the many young plants that will eventually provide us with spring colour. Low temperatures combined with decreasing daylight hours and unavoidable dampness in the air call for extreme care in watering, and full advantage of the few sunny days must be taken by admitting sensible amounts of fresh air through the top ventilators on every possible occasion. Collar rot is the enemy this month and calceolarias and primulas in particular need very minimal waterings, just sufficient to prevent flagging or the complete drying out of the soil ball. Any decaying lower leaves must be removed with a sharp knife, and scratching over the soil surface in pots with a sharp split cane will prevent sourness and beneficially admit air to the roots.

Pots of annual plants can now be disposed of and the soil, if allowed to dry out, will easily shake away. It amounts to well over 1 tonne and we stack ours outside to 'weather' for the winter. In the early spring it is put through a 12mm (½ in) riddle and a 15cm (6in) potful of bonemeal is added to every 36 litres (1 bushel). This makes good top dressing for the rock garden, primrose bed and lawns.

Inevitably, empty pots pile up and a real effort must be made now to clean and store them away. An old 1m (3ft) deep water tank is ideal for this task and a dessert-spoon full of Jeyes Fluid should be added to every 4.5 litres (1gal) of water. Plastic pots present no problems, they clean perfectly with a pot brush and dry within half an hour. Clay pots, on the other hand, need a thorough soaking to loosen the salt deposit just below the rim and consequently require elbow grease and a wire brush to remove it.

It is never too early to commence the routine cleaning and washing down of all glasshouses, and a thorough check should be made for loose or broken glass before the approach of severe weather. Badly cracked glass should preferably be replaced, but if conditions are not suitable a very sound repair job can be carried out with a puttied tape available in varying widths. Make sure that all windows fit flush to their frames, and this applies to doors also – it is surprising just how much valuable heat can be lost in this way.

Whilst there is plenty of room on the benches I find it an excellent time to sow seeds of alpine plants which have been collected in the past few weeks. Pans are filled to a third of their depth with drainage material and topped with 2.5cm (1in) of coarse leafmould, followed by a well drained seed compost to within 12mm (½ in) of the rim.

Pans of alpine seeds sown in December plunged in a north facing ash bed. Exposure to frost greatly assists germination in the early spring

My own choice is equal parts of sterilised loam, peat and sharp gritty sand, and once the seeds have been sown they are topped with a 6mm (¼ in) layer of fine poultry grit. The pans are placed in an open frame and covered only in periods of persistent rain; indeed, some varieties, *Codonopsis*, hellebores, gentians and campanulas to name a few – are greatly assisted in germination by being frozen. On no account should plantless pans be thrown out after the first winter, as so often after a year's cycle of dormancy seeds will germinate freely the following year.

I personally find raising the more uncommon plants from seed to be one of the most satisfying sides of horticulture. In some cases it is the only successful method of increase, and of course there is always that remote chance of the once-in-a-lifetime hybrid.

On reflection, it has been a difficult year in the kitchen garden, in that the cold wet spring was not at all conducive to the raising of early vegetables. At the same time nature has a wonderful way of compensating, and when growing conditions eventually arrived they were extremely good. The practical answer is protected cultivation, in the form of cloches or frames. Whilst glass is certainly the best material it is also very expensive and opens the field to imaginative ideas using plastics. Strong wire hoops covered with medium gauge plastic sheeting can form an excellent growing tunnel as long as both ends are sealed to prevent wind channeling, and they can be easily moved to adjacent crops when necessary. In a year such as this, all forms of protection have more than proved their worth, advancing crops by at least a month and, in the case of salad vegetables, by six or seven weeks. Such protection helps to bridge the gap between sprouting broccoli, late leeks, spring cauliflower and winter lettuce, and the first of the early summer crops, and any fresh vegetable at this time is a valuable bonus.

At last we start digging leeks. They are in prime condition and will be in great demand over the Christmas period. When cooked perfectly fresh, they are certainly a beautiful vegetable. In fact, they cause me a slight problem, as once they find their way into the kitchen, other vegetables become somewhat neglected, and as head gardener it is my responsibility to keep the supply of fresh vegetables as varied as possible.

Sharp frost has kept the Brussels sprouts tight and firm and parsnips are sweet as nuts; Autumn King carrots now suffer from slug damage but there are sufficient for table use; cabbage Christmas Drumhead has for once matured as its name suggests; the last of the swedes are lifted and we still have fresh parsley from under cloches.

There are just two more varieties of apple to be picked this month, Laxton's Superb and Winston. In both cases they benefit by being left on the tree until the last possible moment. Our Laxton's Superb are old trees, much branched and spreading and forming an effective windbreak for younger trees in the top orchard. They are biennial bearing and carry very heavy crops of fruit every other year. Colour is russet red on a pale green background but the flavour is rather dull, and only fruit at the tops of the trees bear any briskness. Although widely grown for a late dessert apple, it is very prone to scab in chalky soils and would not be my choice in future plantings. Winston, on the other hand, is a really first-class late apple and a great improvement on Laxton's Superb in flavour and texture. The slightly smaller fruit are carried freely over the whole tree, the skin is highly flushed and apt to be on the thick side as the month progresses, yet the flesh is juicy with a musky sweetness. Its excellent keeping qualities make this apple a very valuable all-round variety and it is my first choice for a late dessert.

Severe frosts towards the end of the month have made winter digging almost impossible, but we are in the fortunate position of having completed the cultivation of all vacant ground. It is so essential that the maximum surface area is fully exposed to frost in the months to come to give us a workable tilth in the early spring. Stocks of farmyard manure and compost are now somewhat depleted but sufficient remains to top dress most of the flower borders.

Once again it is pruning time, and during milder spells in the next two months all our fruit trees in various forms will be pruned for shape as well as for encouraging the renewal of young fruiting spurs. I must also emphasise that fruit trees, both young and old, will respond to feeding and summer irrigation by producing good-quality fruit; so often they are neglected and taken for granted. Soft fruit are much quicker to show soil deficiencies and again will only carry quality fruit if attention is paid to their needs.

So often in professional gardening, time is the deciding and key factor in conjunction with available labour. In a work-intensive garden such as ours, it is very easy to overlook the individual attention that many subjects require, and for this reason it is sound practice to keep a written record of pruning, cropping rotas and manuring, thus ensuring that all, perhaps over a period of two years, receive assistance to meet the demands of our hungry soil.

Inevitably, there is one month of the year when colour almost disappears from the garden. By this I mean colour of actual flowers, yet once deciduous subjects have shed their leaves coloured bark and stems, seldom seen during summer, play an important role. The silhouettes of fastigiate and weeping trees are often quite beautiful against an ice-blue winter sky, and the bog garden, now denuded of giant foliage plants, is starkly outlined by uncongested paths of clear running water. *Cornus*, in particular, give welcome colour to the shrub border; the red-stemmed cultivars such as *C. alba* Spaethii and Westonbirt combined with the mustard-yellow *Castolonifera* Flaviramea are very pleasing, never more so than when winter sun brings the stems to life.

The evergreen greys such as *Phlomis fruticosa, Ballota pseudodictamnus* and *Senecio laxifolius* remain in good leaf condition until the end of this month but are often nipped by severe frost after

Christmas. Perhaps the most eye catching of all plants in a winter garden is *Iris foetidissima* Variegata, perpetually bright with its longitudinally striped green and cream handsome leaves. Slow to increase and needing a lightly shaded position to show off the striking foliage to its best, it is nevertheless a fine plant deservedly accorded the Award of Merit and Award of Garden Merit.

We have tried phormiums this year, and if they prove hardy under our conditions more will be planted. I have always admired them for their brilliantly coloured foliage and focal individuality, and we hope that the two varieties on trial, Cream Delight and Dark Delight will be the fore-runners of many more.

Both *Cotoneaster* Exburiensis and *C.* × *watereri* are still well berried, and other species show delightful russet tints to their leaves. A small tree of great interest that is surprisingly hardy here is *Mahonia lomariifolia*. A native of Yunnan Province, China, it is one of the most imposing of its genus with strong erect branches and long foliage composed of fifteen or more pairs of leaflets. The upright racemes of yellow flowers are borne in the terminal clusters and appear from midwinter onwards. Although open to the north winds, it has the backing of a tall wall and some protection from surrounding trees, and in summer has the quite dense shade which it insists on.

The season of the viburnum is with us once more. *Viburnum fragrans* bears the first crop of scented flowers that fill the air in a still day with sweet fragrance, and *V. tinus*, along with its variegated counterpart *V. t.* Variegatum, are quietly attractive with their dense pink and white flower heads that can open off and on for most of late winter. The loosely barked stems of *V.* × *bodnantense* Dawn are again loaded with clusters of pink buds and will be a picture in a week or two. In the woodland, *Prunus subhirtella* Autumnalis and the pink form *P. s.* A. Rosea are dotted with blossom that intermittently opens through to March. Not spectacular, this is still a very useful winter flowering tree, seen at its best when incorporated with mixed plantings.

Yellow is a warming colour on a winter's day and never more charmingly presented than on *Jasminum nudiflorum*, which flowers profusely and unceasingly in all weathers. Undeservedly, it is sometimes shrugged at as being a nuisance, yet with hard pruning after flowering it can be trained and kept in bounds. Without doubt it is one of the most colourful winter flowering subjects that can be grown.

Conifers of course, supply the real depth of colour to the winter garden and, with careful forethought, can provide unlimited all-the-year-round interest. I am not quite sure just why they have not been more widely planted here in the past, and one of my first priorities on arrival here was to start to introduce some of the many fine cultivars that are available nowadays. Apart from the avenue of *Chamaecyparis lawsoniana* Columnaris Glauca across the main lawn and some very large sprawling *Juniperus* × *media* Pfitzerana Aurea at the head of the rock garden, there were few others to be seen. The shallow and stony topsoil perhaps is not the best encouragement, but once the root system has delved into the moist brash underlay the trees will grow away rapidly. Preparation of the site is all important and a sizeable hole must be taken out and large stones removed. The incorporation of peat and organic material will greatly add to the moisture-holding factors that are vitally important in the first two years of a conifer's life, and watering is necessary in hot summers following planting.

A few varieties of *Cedrus* and *Pinus* are not too happy on alkaline soils but the choice of conifers still remains varied and almost unending. Extremely valuable at this time of the year are the 'golds', which, where possible, should be planted against a darker background to accentuate their beautiful winter colouring. A favourite of mine is *Chamaecyparis lawsoniana* Stardust; its closely set golden foliage is outstanding and the narrow erect habit makes it a first class focal conifer. Where space is available *Cupressocyparis leylandii* Castlewellen Gold makes a fine upright specimen, growth is strong and rapid and the colouring changes with the seasons from bronzy gold to sulphur yellow. The coppery tints of *Thuja plicata* Semperaurescens this month are most effective, and as spring approaches the tips turn bright gold. Needing a year or two to show its true form is the slender *Juniperus scopulorum* Skyrocket, a smoky grey cultivar especially valuable as an accent plant. The real gems, in my opinion, are the medium-sized forms, loosely called dwarf but containing varieties of upright and spreading habit in diverse colourings. In time, *Cryptomeria japonica* Elegans will make a soft rounded 'tree', but no other conifer is more striking in winter: the feathery foliage turns from a lime green to truly indescribable tints of purple, plum and russet red. Ideal for the rock garden is *C. j.* Vilmoriniana, which grows into a dense dark green dome and takes on rusty hues in winter.

Other varieties that I have recently planted in the rock garden are *Chamaecyparis* Blue Nantais, a conical slow growing form with marvellous silvery summer tints; *C. lawsoniana* Minima Aurea which is an outstanding year-round gold; and *C. lawsoniana* Gimbornii, a metallic blue of rounded and compact habit. The junipers provide some excellent forms also; *Juniperus* × *media* Old Gold, *J. squamata* Blue Star and *J. s.* Blue Carpet are all semi-prostrate and worthy of inclusion in any garden. Tumbling over a large rock, *J. virginiana* Grey Owl, a prostrate grey-blue form contrasts well with the limy greyness of Westmorland stone. The real miniatures include *Abies balsamea* Hudsonia, *Picea abies* Nidiformis and the smallest of all, *Picea mariana* Nana. One thing for sure, in the next few years I shall annually add many more conifers of varying forms to our garden.

Meanwhile there is a vast amount of routine tidying work to be completed. Bush and floribunda roses must be topped to minimise movement in the ground during strong winds, decaying leaves must be removed from herbaceous plants and at the same time old stems cut back to 30cm (1ft), giving that little protection from frost and snow. Blowing leaves seem to be in every corner and must be collected. With the exception of magnolia, which does not decompose easily, they are all composted or stacked in netted bins for use as a mulch or long term potting soil ingredient.

The avenue of lime trees need pleaching to keep them to shape and size. This consists of shortening back the current year's growth to two buds and at the same time intertwining lateral growths to form a dense screen.

There is no close season in professional gardening, an abundance of work is ever present and must be tackled as and when the weather conditions permit. I am indeed, a fortunate man, and I am sure I voice the opinion of my capable staff when I say it is sheer joy to be involved in a garden such as ours and to devote most of one's life to a complex and perpetually challenging career.

LIST OF PLANTS

The following is a list of selected plants growing at Cornwell Manor and chosen by the author as being of outstanding merit and highly suitable for alkaline soils.

HERBACEOUS PLANTS

Achillea taygetea Moonshine
Agapanthus campanulatus Albus
Alstroemeria ligtu hybrids
Artemisia nutans
Aster amellus Violet Queen
Aster spectabilis
Astrantia Margery Fish
Campanula lactiflora Pritchard's Var.
Centaurea pulchra major
Cimicifuga racemosa
Coreopsis verticillata Grandiflora
Crocosmia Lucifer & Spitfire
Dicentra spectabilis
Digitalis × *mertonensis*
Doronicum Spring Beauty
Echinops ritro
Eryngium tripartitum
Euphorbia polychroma
Geranium sylvaticum Album
Heliopsis scabra Golden Plume
Hosta fortunei Aureomarginata
Iris foetidissima Variegata
Iris tectorum

Linum narbonense
Lychnis viscaria Splendens Plena
Morina longifolia
Oenothera glaber
Paeonia mlokosewitschii
Paeonia lactiflora Sarah Bernhardt
Penstemon hartwegii Garnet
Phlox paniculata Vintage Wine
Phlox White Admiral
Polygonum Arun Gem
Potentilla Wm Rollison
Pulmonaria Rob Roy
Pyrethrum roseum James Kelway
Rudbeckia Deamii
Salvia East Friesland
Scabiosa caucasica Clive Greaves
Scabiosa graminifolia Pink Cushion
Sedum × Autumn Joy
Sedum maximum Atropurpureum
Sidalcea Rose Queen
Solidago Goldenmosa
Thalictrum dipterocarpum
Verbascum hybridum Cotswold Queen

ALPINE AND ROCK PLANTS

Achillea Kolbiana
Aethionema × Warley Rose
Androsace sarmentosa Sherriffii
Anthyllis montana Rubra
Artemisia glacialis
Aubretia Dr Mules
Campanula carpatica Isobel
Campanula Peter Nix
Dianthus Inchmery
Dianthus Pikes Pink
Diascia Ruby Field
Gentiana verna Angulosa
Geranium Ballerina
Geranium subcaulescens
Gypsophila Dorothy Teacher
Helianthemum lunulatum
Helianthemum Wisley Primrose
Hypericum Coris
Iberis sempervirens Little Gem
Linum capitatum
Linum Gemmel's Hybrid

Origanum laevigatum
Penstemon Pink Dragon
Phlox douglasii Rose Queen
Phlox subulata Marjory
Platycodon grandiflorus Apoyama
Pulsatilla vulgaris Rubra
Saxifraga Esther
Saxifraga × Jenkinsae
Scutellaria scordifolia
Sedum cauticolum
Sedum × Ruby Glow
Sisyrinchium macounii Album
Teucrium ackermanii
Thymus Anderson's Gold
Thymus Doone Valley
Veronica Heidekind
Veronica rupestris
Viola hederacea
Viola Irish Molly
Zauschneria californica Dublin

GRASSES

Avena candida
Carex variegata Aurea
Cortaderia Gold Band
Hakonechloa macra Albo-aurea
Lasiogrostis splendens

Miscanthus Silver Feather
Miscanthus sinensis Zebrinus
Molinia caerulea Variegata
Panicum milliaceum
Stipa gigantea

FLOWERING SHRUBS

Berberis thunbergii Aurea
Berberis thunbergii Rose Glow
Buddleia davidii Royal Red
Caryopteris clandonensis
Ceanothus Gloire de Versailles
Choisya ternata
Cornus alba Elegantissima
Corylopsis spicata
Cotoneaster franchetii
Cytisus kewensis

Cytisus praecox
Deutzia pulchra
Forsythia Lynwood
Fuchsia Mrs Popple
Genista lydia
Hypericum Hidcote
Lavandula angustifolia Hidcote
Mahonia japonica
Osmanthus delavayi
Potentilla arbuscula Abbotswood

Potentilla Daydawn
Potentilla Elizabeth
Potentilla Goldfinger
Potentilla Vilmoriniana
Salix hastata Wehrhahnii

Salvia officinalis Icterina
Spiraea × *bumalda* Goldflame
Syringa palibiniana
Viburnum × *bodnantense* Dawn
Viburnum × *burkwoodii*

CLIMBERS

Actinidia kolomikta
Akebia quinata
Chaenomeles speciosa Simonii
Clematis macropetala
Hedera helix Tricolor
Hydrangea petiolaris

Jasminum nudiflorum
Lonicera periclymenum Belgica
Pyracantha Orange Glow
Vitis vinifera Brant
Wisteria sinensis
Wisteria sinensis Alba

WATERSIDE

Aruncus sylvester
Astilbes
Gunnera manicata
Ligularia Desdemona
Lobelia cardinalis

Primula, candelabra and
    sikkimensis section
Rheum palmatum
Schizostylis coccinea

MEDIUM-SIZED TREES

Acer griseum
Acer negundo Variegatum
Catalpa bignonioides
Cotoneaster × *Watereri*
Fagus sylvatica Rohanii
Laburnum × *watereri* Vossii
Malus floribunda
Malus Profusion
Prunus sargentii

Prunus Shidare Sakura
Prunus Shirofugen
Parrotia persica
Pyrus salicifolia Pendula
Salix caprea
Sorbus intermedia
Syringa vulgaris Maud Notcutt
Viburnum rhytidophyllum

188

INDEX

Numbers in *italics* indicate illustrations